MW01001042

S·M·A·L·L WORLDS

S·M·A·L·L WORLDS

Communities of Living Things

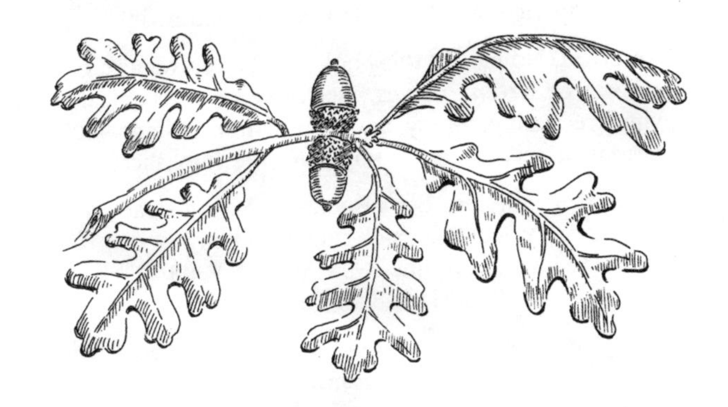

Written and Illustrated by
HOWARD E. SMITH, JR.

CHARLES SCRIBNER'S SONS
NEW YORK

The author wishes to express his gratitude to Dr. Andrew Spielman, Medical Entomologist, Harvard School of Public Health, for his generosity of time and spirit in making comments on the manuscript of this book.

Copyright © 1987 by Howard E. Smith, Jr.

All rights reserved. No part of this book may be reproduced or transmitted in any form or by any means, electronic or mechanical, including photocopying, recording, or by any information storage and retrieval system, without permission in writing from the Publisher.

Charles Scribner's Sons Books for Young Readers
Macmillan Publishing Company
866 Third Avenue, New York, NY 10022
Collier Macmillan Canada, Inc.

Printed in the United States of America
First Edition
10 9 8 7 6 5 4 3 2 1

Library of Congress Cataloging-in-Publication Data
Smith, Howard Everett, Jr., date Small worlds.
Summary: Describes a number of small self-contained communities, including a sand dune, tidal pool, old barn, and vacant lot, and examines the ways in which the plants and animals interact.
Includes index.
1. Biotic communities—Juvenile literature.
2. Ecology—Juvenile literature.
[1. Biotic communities. 2. Ecology] I. Title.
QH541.14.S65 1987 574.5 87-9856
ISBN 0-684-18723-X

In memory of my father,
who taught me how to see nature

Contents

S·M·A·L·L WORLDS

What Is an Ecosystem?

Life takes on millions of shapes from starfish to pine trees, from bread molds to robins, from crabs to daisies. There are over a million different species of plants and about half a million species of animals. Each species is different. Moreover, each individual plant and animal is in some ways different from its relatives, even its closest relatives. Untold numbers of plants and animals live on earth, each a unique individual.

Each plant and animal has its own place on earth, its territory, its home.

Take your own yard or a nearby park, for example. It probably has been visited by two thousand species of insects. Almost certainly it contains or has been visited by such insects as fireflies, praying mantises, huge io moths, migrating monarch butterflies, hawkmoths, ants, fleas, cabbage butterflies, swallowtail butterflies, ladybugs, ground beetles, soldier beetles, and so on. The list is almost endless. Dozens of species of birds have visited it, without doubt house wrens, juncos, finches, pigeons, sparrow hawks, robins, many different kinds of warblers, sparrows, and many other species of birds. Mammals have been in it, too: mice, moles, cats, dogs, rats, squirrels, shrews, not to mention your family, and friends. In the ground and in the trees, there are countless billions of tiny living beings: worms, sow bugs, spiders, termites, fungi, algae, bacteria, and microscopic animals. The air over the yard contains pollens (some might make you sneeze and your eyes water).

Life is far more common than we might imagine it to be. It can be found in the deepest oceans, in dry deserts, but also under your sink and in the soil. Most plants and animals have plants and animals living on them and in them. Even little fleas have bacteria, single-celled animals, and viruses in them.

Because life is so common, it is always easy to find—even for the city dweller. All a city dweller has to do is go to the nearest tree or the nearest vacant lot or park to find hundreds of fascinating plants and animals. Trees, parks, and yards are small worlds almost complete in themselves.

Outside of the city there are many more small worlds: the sand dunes on the beach, the tidal pools along the rocky coast, the cliffs on hills, canyons, and mountains, and stray boulders. There are barns to explore, not just for horses, cows, goats, and chickens, but also for wild animals such as insects, snakes, bats, mice, barn swallows, owls, and spiders and others.

These small worlds are there to be explored, and nothing can quite equal one's own explorations of them. Life is always fascinating and worth investigating, for life is beauty and excitement and vitality. Most of all, life is pleasing to us, for we ourselves are alive and share this world with plants and animals.

If you do explore for new plants and animals, which is so

easily done, you will soon find that life varies greatly from place to place.

The explorer will soon discover that in a vacant lot, for example, some plants grow only in the shade. Others will grow where they can get a great deal of sunlight. (Anyone who has grown houseplants will know that some plants need shade, others some sunlight, and others lot and lots of sunlight.) Some insects will feed only on certain plants and not others. Some birds will always stay in the treetops and never be seen on the grass. Others will almost always stay on the ground. Each little place, even in one vacant lot, will have its own plants and animals.

These plants and animals set up **communities***. The plants, for example, grow only in certain communities, such as vacant lots, fields, seashores, on sand dunes, or in wet, damp places. They grow where the light, rain, and soil are best for them. They grow where there is not too much cold or heat. Some plants thrive in cool places, others in warm places. Plants are very particular about where they live.

Most animals eat plants, so they go where the plants are, and because they are finicky eaters and often will feed from only a certain type of plant or on certain seeds or sip only nectar, they gather around the plants they need. The animals must also choose their climate, in terms of sunlight and shade, temperature extremes, and much, much more. **Predators** must, in turn, always be near the animals they hunt.

Communities of plants and animals anywhere are all similar in one way. The plants determine the community. The

---

*Words set in boldface type are defined in the glossary on pages 171-74.

plant-eating animals stay near certain plants, and the predators—be they lions, sharks, or praying mantises—must be where the plant-eating animals gather. In all small worlds, and larger ones as well, the three exist together: plants, plant eaters, predators.

All these living beings must find some way of dealing with one another. There are the hunters and the hunted. Birds eat insects. Snakes eat spiders and worms. Many insects hunt other insects. Wolf spiders hunt. Other spiders wait in their webs. Praying mantises wait to catch insects.

Strange as it may seem at first, there is a struggle taking place among the plants themselves. Each plant fights constantly with other plants for water, for soil, for sunlight. Some plants, such as fungi, directly attack other plants. On one acre of land, thousands of seeds fall on the ground each year, but very few will sprout. Fewer still will become fully grown plants. Most plants are defeated, not by animals, but by other plants, which take away valuable water, crowd the soil with roots, or grow in the sunlight and kill other plants with their shade. In any small world—a vacant lot, a tidal pool, even a single tree—one can see some of this struggle taking place.

Living things struggle, too, with the physical world itself. All living things need to adjust to the air and earth. Plants must grow in the right soil—not too sandy, too limy, too filled with humus. A cactus needs sandy soil; violets need rich, damp soil; some ferns grow only near or on limestone. Each plant must find its own type of soil or it will never develop. Plants and animals must struggle, too, with the climate: hot summers, cold winters, too much or not enough wind, heavy rains, drier climates, and so on.

Many animals—insects and snakes, for example—must

be able to sun themselves when it is cool and find shade when it is hot. Some predators must find places to hide and wait for prey; others need open spaces where they can easily see their prey.

Fortunately, not everything is a struggle. Most of the time, plants and animals coexist peacefully and beautifully. In all places, living things cooperate with one another, although the cooperation, is, of course, mostly unconscious. Tall trees provide needed shade for wild flowers. Bees cooperate with flowers by taking nectar and carrying pollen away. Predators eat mice and thus protect plants from the sharp teeth of the mice. Insects and birds that eat mosquitoes protect us from their bites. In each small world, and in large ones, too, there are numerous helpful, even vital, relationships between plants and animals.

The study of the struggles and cooperative relationships between plants and animals and the physical world they live in is called ecology. The small worlds are often called small **ecosystems**.

Life on planet earth is balanced. For almost a billion years, and perhaps longer, plants and animals have balanced each other out. Even in small worlds plants and animals also balance each other. Each, in its own way, gives life to the other.

In reality, plants and animals need each other. We are all on this lovely planet earth together. No plant or animal can live alone; no human being can live alone either.

Some schools have set up an interesting fishbowl experiment. In a water-filled bowl are placed water plants—such as tape grass (*Vallisneria*), water foxtail (*Myriophyllum*) or *Elodea,* also called *Anacharis*—and some fish, usually goldfish. The fishbowl is sealed tightly so that no air, or anything else, can get into it or out of it. The fish survive by eating part of the plants. As they breathe with their gills they exhale carbon dioxide. The plants use the carbon dioxide. Green **chlorophyll**, which gives the plants their color, manufactures food for the plants from the water, sunlight, and carbon dioxide, which was received from the fish. As the plants make food for themselves with the chlorophyll in a process called **photosynthesis**, they give off oxygen as a byproduct, which the fish will use when they breathe. The droppings of the fish help fertilize the plants by providing their soil with nitrogen compounds and needed minerals.

Such a closed fishbowl is an ideal small world. The fish and plants set up a relationship that benefits them both. They recycle needed life-giving oxygen and carbon dioxide from one to the other. They also recycle nitrogen compounds (needed for proteins) and minerals from one to the other. In doing so, the fish and plants sustain each other's life. Life in such a fishbowl can continue for a couple of years or more. It is one of the smallest self-contained living worlds we know of.

A much larger self-contained ecosystem is planned for a two-and-one-half acre area in Arizona, near the town of Oracle. A house, fishponds, and garden will be built under glass and sealed like the fishbowl by Decisions Team, Ltd. The place will have trees, fish, garden plants, and—most interesting of all—human volunteers. The glass enclosure will be sealed for two years, and during that time the volunteers will not leave except in an emergency. For the first time ever, humans will live in a true small world. They will eat plant food and fish and in turn will fertilize the gardens with their own waste products. (Farmers in Asia have fertilized their gardens this way for centuries.) The plants will provide oxygen, and the humans and fish will provide carbon dioxide for the plants. If all goes well, the small world will show us more about how plants, animals, and humans live together in small worlds.

The idea of sealing people into an environment seems unnerving; yet, when one thinks about it, the truth is that we are all sealed into an environment called planet earth. In the vastness of space it is but a dot, a very small world indeed.

This book is about the ecology of small worlds, but the book is not intended to be an end in itself. Quite the opposite. It is intended to give you ideas so that you can explore the many small worlds waiting just beyond your doorstep.

·1·

An Old House

Quite often thousands of animals live in houses, especially in old houses. We do not usually see them, for they live in hidden places, but they are there—behind walls, under refrigerators, in old trunks, in the dark damp corners of basements and dry dusty corners of attics, and in the very wood that supports the houses.

Old houses are protected, special small worlds. Of course, no small world is closer to us. It is our own world, one that we share with all those creatures.

Let us take for example an old house, at least three hundred years old, built someplace in one of the original thirteen colonies. When one thinks of an old house as a small world, one first notices the people living in the house. The house helps them survive. It serves as a shelter from cold winds in the winter and as a shaded place in the summer. Once, long ago, the house helped keep out bears, skunks, and rattlesnakes. It is a place where people can store their belongings and food. In terms of survival this is important, for humans need special equipment for cooking, for medicines, for keeping clean, and in the old days for storing weapons for hunting and possibly for defense. The beds assure people of a good night's rest, so that they can face life less fatigued. It is a place where a person can be comfortably sick for a few days and have a chance to recover. It is a safe place for childbirth. The screens of the house (since the nineteenth century) serve the important purpose of keeping out insects, a few of which may carry deadly diseases. In these ways and many others, the house serves as an environment important for human survival.

Originally, most old houses were surrounded by farmland. They were places of business—the business of farming. Families grew corn, wheat, and rye to eat as well as to sell for cash. They used the cash for tools, medicines, rum, hardware, and shoes.

The house, the land, and the large society beyond, which could supply such things as tea, fabrics, nails, pistols, sugar, and similar goods, made the family self-sufficient. The farm served as a true small world for a family.

Much as plants and animals adapt to their small worlds, the family adapted to theirs. But there was a difference. Plants and animals can at best make only small changes (such as digging holes or building nests) in their worlds. Humans constantly changed theirs. Over the centuries different families have changed old houses, usually improving them—with window screens, for example, and air conditioners, central heating, and larger windows that let in more light.

The next most noticeable inhabitants of the house are the dogs and cats. A dog will guard a house and serve as a companion and playmate for the children. As we will see later, dogs may also interact with insects, which may or may not bite the people of the house. Cats play a more active biologic role in the small world of a house than dogs do, hunting mice and sometimes large insects.

The next most noticeable animals are the birds. When the first settlers arrived on the land, nothing existed there but a forest. Many different species of birds lived in the forest. Once the trees had been cut and land cleared for the growing of crops, the forest birds moved away. New species of birds that preferred fields moved onto the land. When the house and barn went up, other types of birds arrived.

Considering that there were, and are, literally hundreds of species of birds in the original thirteen colonies, it is surprising how few will tolerate close living with humans. About a dozen or so species do. Those that nest in buildings and do not mind the constant activity of people coming and going, talking, and even shouting, have thrived.

The original settlers, knowing that swallows eat great numbers of insect pests, encouraged swallows to live on their land. Barn and cliff swallows make mud nests under the eaves of houses and barns. Today some people do not want the birds around because of the mud and droppings, but for centuries they were most welcome.

Rapidly flying swallows hunt insects in the air. Twisting and turning, they can easily catch them. An average swallow flies hundreds of miles a day. Circling about, back and forth it goes, but only a few miles from its nest.

For beauty few birds can outdo bluebirds. In certain lights an eastern bluebird can flash one of the most gorgeous blue colors in nature. Nesting on exposed beams of the house, on attic windowsills, and other such places, bluebirds were welcomed by early settlers. Today, unfortunately, the bluebird population is on the decline because starlings have taken over many of their nesting places, driving them out.

In the late nineteenth century some people who longed

to see English birds in our countryside brought over starlings and let them loose. It was a terrible ecological mistake. Today starlings trouble the countryside. Their flocks can be huge, numbering in the hundreds of thousands. They either attack or drive away desired native species of birds from their nesting grounds, and eat tens of millions of dollars worth of wheat and other crops. They foul houses, streets, and park lands. Starlings increased in America because they have no powerful natural enemies here to keep down their populations.

Almost anyone today can find starlings near a house. They often show up unexpectedly and flock about, eating whatever they can find. Ivy berries, for example, often attract them. After eating ripe berries, they leave and go on. The flocks raid, disappear, and raid again weeks or months later.

Chimney swifts often make nests in chimneys. These swifts are less common today because many houses lack chimneys, but one can still see them in the summertime around a few houses. Well-named, the birds can show remarkable displays of speed as they cut gracefully through the air. On the wing, they, too, hunt flying insects. If one remembers that they are often called cigars with wings, it is easy to identify them.

Little house wrens act pert and saucy. No bird finds itself more at home, more willing to nest someplace on a house—under a gable, under a gutter, in vines—as the house wren. These little birds are plump and have stiff upright tails. They have a gushing, bubbly song, which to our ears sounds joyous and happy. Since they eat only insects and spiders, they are welcome to most householders.

English sparrows, like starlings, came here from Europe

with human help. Strictly speaking, they are not sparrows but finches. One can easily identify the males; they are the only common sparrowlike birds with black "bibs" under their bills. English sparrows act with more intelligence than some mammals. They can be trapped once in a particular type of trap, but never again, for they learn to avoid it.

A house wren

Amazingly, they will follow and "study" predators, such as rats and cats, to learn their hunting techniques and see how to avoid them. Each English sparrow is protected by the entire flock. If one bird sees danger it calls out and all take off.

English sparrows eat leftovers: bits of grain, crusts of bread, spilled popcorn. No other bird does this to the same degree. When they came to America the English sparrows filled what is called a niche in the ecosystem. That is, they alone of all birds utilized a particular kind of opportunity given them by the settlers, namely the presence of leftover food dropped on the ground. (Native American Indians had little trash. Civilization produces it by the millions of tons, more than enough for the birds.)

Unlike bluebirds, swallows, wrens, and swifts, the English sparrows winter in all of our states south of Canada. These hardy birds can take cold weather, and because they stay in one place they learn that place well and have survival advantages. They save energy in the springtime because they neither have to migrate nor build new nests. Last year's nest, perhaps with a few repairs, will do. As a result, there is less room for other nesting birds because as the English sparrow population expands, so does the number of their permanent nesting places.

So far, we've mentioned only the most-easily-seen animals. Among the hidden ones are the mice. It is difficult to keep them out of any house because there is an intimate relationship between humans and mice that has lasted for thousands of years. Though people can easily and beneficially live without mice, the opposite is not true. House mice could not exist without close contact with humans. Actually, they are about as dependent on us as dogs are. Very rarely, and only with great luck, can a dog or a house mouse survive in the wilds.

Zoologists call the relationship between mice and humans in a house **commensalism,** meaning "sharing the same table." How true that is. Mice obtain their food from what we drop from the table or let fall behind a refrigerator or leave unprotected.

Unlike a field mouse, the ordinary house mouse is a native not of America but of the steppes of Russia. To the householder, the biggest difference between the two is the fact that American field mice rarely enter houses. On the other hand, the house mouse is almost never found anyplace but in a house or a barn. Another big difference is that American field mice are much cleaner than house mice. Fleas that bite the mice and then bite humans may transmit diseases. The fleas on mice, cats, dogs, and humans, by the way, are also part of the small world of a house, new or old. If the fleas carry deadly bacteria-caused diseases and tapeworms, as they sometimes do, then they are an extremely important part of the small world of a house.

As anyone who has watched house mice in action knows, they quickly and with amazing ease find their way around a house. This is so because mice thoroughly learn their pathways in houses. They also remember the location of furniture and other objects. In this way they differ from rats. If a new piece of furniture appears along a path that a rat takes, the rat will often turn around and leave. Not a mouse. Mice become curious about new objects. Carefully and nervously a mouse will investigate a new object in its familiar pathway. It will go around it and check it out from all sides, looking at it, touching it, and smelling it. Once satisfied that it is not dangerous, the mouse will relearn the pathway and take the new object into account.

A house mouse learns pathways and routes across a floor, not by visually remembering them, but by learning them kinesthetically. We know that we have five senses: sight, touch, hearing, smell, taste. Actually we possess another sense as well. We have a knowledge of, and a memory of, muscle movements. Even in darkness, for instance, we can bring two fingers together in front of us and touch one against the other.

A house mouse learns to run from a hole, past a chair,

and over to a passageway behind a chest of drawers, by its kinesthetic sense. It memorizes each muscle movement involved when taking the dash. This gives the house mouse great advantages. If a cat appears, the mouse just keeps running, each step and each leap having already been memorized. It will not make a single mistake.

House mice moved in and began living with humans thousands of years ago. They will probably live with us forever.

Another animal likely to live in an old house at one time or another is a bat. Those found in houses are usually either big brown bats or little brown bats. Before settlers came to the New World, big and little brown bats roosted in caves, in hollow trees, and in other such natural shelters. When settlers built houses, barns, and churches, especially those with steeples, bats found new places to roost. Ever since they have roosted in buildings, in out of the way places such as attics, storerooms, and even basements.

For some unknown reason, most people fear bats and find them distasteful. That is unfortunate. Actually bats cause no harm and do a great deal of good. They have evolved their strange looks and ways so that they can survive utter darkness and achieve rapid, acrobatic flight. No other mammal comes close to matching them in either respect.

Bats find their way in darkness by means of echoes. High pitched squeaks, too high for us to hear, bounce off walls, trees, clotheslines, and—very important—off insects. Bats hear the returning echoes and thus know what is near them. The echoes are so effective that a bat can easily fly in a dark cave and avoid hitting stalactites and stalagmites and, equally remarkable, other bats. Bats hunt flying insects at night thanks to echolocation. In America they consume literally trillions of insects, many of which are dangerous pests, each year.

In spite of their name, big brown bats are small animals, less than five inches in length. Only a person very familiar with bats could identify a big brown bat, which has a uniform brown color and medium-sized ears. The easiest way to identify these very common bats is by their habits. Not many other species of bats live in houses and fly erratically around streetlights. Interestingly, they sometimes wake up from hibernation in the winter and fly about on warm, gray, dark days, even in December and January. Bats seen at that time are sure to be big brown bats.

Another common bat that may roost in a house and hibernate in it is the little brown bat. It is not much smaller than a big brown bat and it is not uniformly brown. It has a glossy brown back and is buff-gray below.

Though a house may give shelter to a dozen mice and an equal number of bats and birds, two or three cats and dogs, and several humans, it may and probably will be at the same time the home of thousands of insects and spiders, only a few of which are ever seen.

In many houses cockroaches either hide or crawl about. If food and water are available, their numbers might increase, even soar. Cockroaches were on earth before the first dinosaurs appeared. In all that time they've changed very little; they are living fossils.

Cockroach survival depends to a great extent on quick responses. If one tries to slap a cockroach, waves of air moving ahead of the hand alert it and it runs away in a split second, in plenty of time to avoid a swat. The cockroach's antennae have "taste and smelling" organs. A cockroach can squeeze into a crack and sniff and taste the air around with its antennae. It can smell food and know when it is available. Cockroaches usually feed only at night in the darkness, which protects them from some of their enemies, but unfortunately keeping a light on all night will not stop cockroaches from eating.

Though terrible nuisances, cockroaches apparently do not spread deadly diseases. On the other hand, they are dirty and depressingly hard to get rid of. The only good thing one can say for them is that they eat bedbugs.

Few houses today have bedbugs, but long ago, before good insecticides were in use, bedbugs could at times be a great nuisance in any house. They are tiny brown insects, rarely as long as one-third of an inch. They do stay near beds. One can crawl on a sleeping person and bite him, causing a rash.

The average old house will have in it many types of beetles. Beetles are insects that have four wings, the upper wing being more like a hard case than a wing. It covers the lower wing, which is used when a beetle flies, if it does at all. Some do not. Unlike many insects, beetles have chewing mouth parts. (A cockroach is a beetle; so is a ladybug.)

There are more species of beetle—at least 250,000—than any other animal on earth, and there may be that many more yet to be discovered. Among them are the small black carpet beetles that live in the wool of carpets, eating away. They are black and tough to crack open. Wood-boring beetles make deep holes and chambers in wood and lay eggs in the holes. Wormlike larvae may live in the holes for months, even years, before emerging again as adult beetles. Some wood-boring beetles are highly colored and gorgeous.

Among other insects in the small world of a house are

termites, which get into the wood of frames, planking, and sidings and make chambers there. A queen termite, which is much bigger than the others, lives in the chambers and is the center of the colony. Worker termites form the chambers and clean them out. After termites chew and swallow wood, bacteria in their guts digest the cellulose in the wood and provide the termites with food. Male termites have only one duty in life and that is to fertilize the eggs of a female queen. At some time during the year, new queens will grow wings and fly out of holes in the wood of an old house. They are followed by many flying male termites. The luckier males will mate with a fertile female. Such flights at times can be dramatic as dozens, perhaps hundreds, of termites fly out. Sometimes termites can completely destroy a house by hollowing out its supporting studs and beams.

A carpenter ant in a wood hole

Another insect that lives in the wood of a house is the carpenter ant. These make the most remarkable chambers in wood of any American insect. The chambers are, in a sense, works of art, beautifully and delicately formed.

Though ants are more highly evolved insects than termites, their social life also focuses on the life of a queen who rules a colony of ants.

An old house may have several other insects that use chambers in the wood as safe hiding places or who actually use the wood as food. Ichneumon flies hunt some insects that live in the wood. This fly can find hidden insects, apparently by listening to insects in the wood. Next, it pokes a long taillike drill into the wood and lays eggs in the unseen insect. The eggs develop, killing the insect host, and new ichneumon flies emerge.

Silverfish are, like cockroaches, ancient animals. Fossil records show that silverfish existed long, long before the dinosaurs. They can live in damp wood, but during the last few centuries they have preferred to live in books, eating the glue and obtaining moisture from it.

Many old houses have working fireplaces that may give warmth to house crickets. Most people consider house crickets to be pleasant creatures, for the sound of their chirps on a winter's night is quite friendly.

Another kind of sound is made by the deathwatch beetle. If one spends a night alone in an old house, one may hear some pretty strange noises. Many are creaks and groans as wood beams and timbers expand or contract due to heat and humidity, but others are insect noises. One such is made by the deathwatch beetle as it bangs on wood to call its mate. The knocking can be quite eerie. Other insects such as carpenter ants make chewing noises. All these sounds heard in the night can give some people "the spooks."

Mosquitoes enter houses looking for the blood of mammals—cats and dogs and, as we all know, humans. Only female mosquitoes bite. They need the blood so that their eggs will develop. Male mosquitoes obtain nourishment by sipping nectar.

Flies also enter houses seeking food and garbage. They lay their eggs in dung or in rotting meats and vegetables. If they can find such materials in garbage pails they will use them. Flies, which are very dirty creatures, also walk on food, sometimes leaving behind a trail of bacteria that can cause diseases.

Hornets most often build nests in out-of-the-way places in houses. Most old houses have been used for nest building many times over the centuries. The hornets that are most likely to invade a house are either the paper or *Polistes* wasps. Paper wasps make large oval nests that are marvels of design. They are composed of paper, which the wasps make by chewing wood and mixing it with saliva. A nest has many, many small chambers in it, which are used for raising young hornets. *Polistes* (from the Greek word for city dweller) wasps make nests that have been likened to small cities. They are much smaller than those made by the paper hornets but are also made of paper and have chambers in them.

Clothes moths also invade houses. The adult moths, which are small (about one-third of an inch long) and gray-brown-white in color, do not eat woolens. Their small wormlike **larvae** do live in woolens, however, eating them to obtain enough moisture from the wool to supply their need for water. They prefer dirty woolens. Sweat stains and other stains provide them with nitrogen, which can help them make proteins.

If insects were left alone, they would soon take over a house. Fortunately they, like all living beings, must battle for survival. We can be thankful that many animals eat insects. Spiders catch insects in their webs and devour them. Daddy longlegs also hunt. Ichneumon flies seek wood-boring insects. Some wasps prey on insects. Cockroaches eat bedbugs. Bats in a house will eat insects. Viruses and bacteria kill vast numbers of insects, and in spite of the fact that houses provide good food sources for insects, many die of starvation. And, of course, most people kill hundreds if not thousands of insects each year with insecticide sprays and traps.

Many unseen life-and-death struggles take place between the animals living in the confines of a house. Sometimes humans are part of the struggle, suffering from insect bites and on occasion from the diseases insects have carried, but rarely these days dying of such diseases.

Among occasional visitors to a house are birds such as pigeons, starlings, and even hawks who might perch on a rooftop for a good view of the surrounding countryside. Butterflies may sip nectar from flowers on house vines or in window flower boxes. Among the most common butterflies are the orange-colored monarchs, large swallowtails, black mourning cloaks, and brown-orange American coppers.

Though some animals are not welcome as residents, others add beauty and charm to the small world of a house, and in the end a house without animals would not be such an interesting place in which to live.

·2·

A Sand Dune

When we think of places hostile to life we are apt to think of far-off, exotic regions, such as the North Pole, high, snow-capped mountains, or the Sahara desert. We do not need to let our minds wander so far. There are places much closer to home that have harsh conditions in which life can barely survive. A sand dune by a beach is an example.

Every aspect of a sand dune works against life. To begin with, strong winds move and shape and build up sand dunes. Year in and year out the very ground moves. On occasion, great storms change the shape of dunes for miles around. A seashore dune may leave its original location and occupy a new one every seventy to eighty years. Because of shifting sands, the roots of plants become either exposed or buried too deeply. Animal holes may also become buried. Winds from the ocean carry salt spray, which very few plants on earth can survive. High winds can carry sand through the air so that it acts like sandpaper, ripping such things as plant leaves and insect wings and irritating the eyes of animals.

Rainwater hardly dampens the sand, because it moves quickly down through the dune. Sand in a dune is not tightly packed. Forty percent of the average dune consists of open spaces between the sand grains. Rainwater races downward through the open spaces. Hardly any dampness, much less water, stays at the surface of the dune. Even those dunes in areas of high rainfall are mostly dry—as dry as desert sands.

In the summer the sand on dunes, even those along our North American coasts, can go to 120°F. Even in New England sand can be much too hot to walk on. Conversely in the winter, the cold sea winds blowing over the dunes can have a wind-chill factor of 50° below zero, even along New York shorelines.

Though so beautiful and white and rounded, dunes are, for life, dreadful places. It is amazing that anything at all lives there. Yet almost all dunes are dotted with plants, and a careful observer can usually discover some animals, too.

Not many types of plants live on dunes, but those that do must adapt to the harsh conditions. They must find some way of modifying themselves so that they can endure on the sand. Let us look at some.

Along the East Coast, a grass called marram grass often grows on dunes. Marram grass grows to be about three feet high. At the top of it are long cylindrical spikes. In almost all ways it must fight for life. Its main problem has to do with the motion of the sand. The wind often blows sand out from under the roots of marram grass. Sometimes small landslides of sand may leave roots exposed to sun and heat. At other times, sand buries the roots. Most grasses would die if their roots were exposed or deeply buried. Actually this is true of marram grass as well. Most parts of the roots of marram grass *do* die off in such cases, but as old roots die, new ones grow quickly by means of runners. These grow just under the sand, moving up to forty feet away to new locations, and from the tips of new sprouts the runners of grass grow upward. The trick of the marram grass is to grow roots fast enough so that new blades of grass can grow high, and thus survive the shifting sands.

Marram grass has to be very tough so that windblown particles of sand do not rip it to pieces or file the leaves or roots away. If you are on a dune, look for a wiry grass about two feet tall. That will be marram grass. Look at its roots and how they hold in the sand. Feel the blades of grass and see how tough they are—but watch out. The blades are sharp.

Marram grass must cope, too, with summer heat. It does this by growing on windy parts of the dunes. Though the surface of a dune may be above 100°F. or more, the windy side is cooler. (Just by noting where marram grass grows, you can tell where the cooler part of the dune is.)

The wind is helpful in another way. The grass slows it down, and as the sand-carrying wind slows down, it drops sand grains near and on the grass. These grains accumulate in time and cover the grass roots, helping the grass to grow.

Marram grass is a native to North America, but there is another common dune plant, dusty miller, which comes from far-off Siberia. It is seen on most of our East Coast sand dunes. Dusty miller has wooly leaves, which are gray-green and covered with white "hairs." In certain lights the plant might look white. When a dusty miller blooms it has a small yellow flower. The leaves are deeply notched. Though a dusty miller might reach a height of two feet, it is often much shorter, frequently not more than about eight inches high.

Dusty millers adapt to the harsh world of dunes in several ways. The fine hairs on their leaves protect them from the sun and shade the working parts of the leaf from direct sunlight. The hairs also protect the leaf from wind-driven sand since sand grains, instead of hitting the delicate leaf, hit the hairs and bounce harmlessly away.

Though marram grass usually grows in the most exposed places of dunes, often along ridges and peaks, dusty miller grows to the lee side of the dunes, mostly out of the reach of sea winds. Moreover, dusty miller grows close to the ground. Dozens, even hundreds of plants will form mats near the ground. Because of their height and location on the dunes, it is difficult for the wind to blow sand away from under them. If they are covered, they will grow higher.

Morning glories often grow on sand dunes, usually in more protected areas, even farther from the reach of the wind and in places where the sand is less likely to move. Like all plants, morning glories have trouble getting water and are helped by their huge roots. When water seeps downward into the sand, the root hairs pick up moisture and carry it to a large, football-shaped root where it is stored.

Some plants, such as lupines, have very long roots. These plants usually have blue flowers that look like the flowers of pea plants (lupines are members of the pea family) and also have leaves that look somewhat like eight fingers in a group, an arrangement called **palmate.** Lupines solve the water problem by sending down many thin, long roots to water below a sand dune. Even though a lupine is rarely over two feet tall, its roots can easily be fifteen feet in length.

Prickly pears, which give some Eastern dunes a South-western look, store water in their leaves. During severe droughts, the leaves are flabby, but after rains, the roots pick up water and store it in the leaves, which then swell and become firm.

Pine trees can and will survive in very dry climates. All plant leaves, including the needles of pines, have tiny holes in them called **stomata.** Gases and water vapor move in and out of stomata. For example, oxygen and water leaving the leaves must move out of the stomata. The more stomata (especially if they are large) a leaf has, the more moisture it will lose when it transpires. Pines needles have few and small stomata. Special cells can close down the stomata, and a waxy substance on the pine needles keeps the needles waterproof so little moisture escapes.

Because they can grow in dry places, some species of pine, usually pitch pines, grow on dunes. Pitch pines are ragged-looking trees. Their short needles come in bundles of three. Pines start growing in protected areas, but sometimes sand covers much of them and then the covered branches and needles die. Yet the uncovered parts of the pine continue to thrive. The upper parts of pine trees often look like young pines when in fact they are merely the tops of tall, very old pines.

Some dune plants, such as white primroses, lose their leaves when conditions are too dry; thus they conserve water because most water loss is through leaves. Many plants tilt their leaves so less sunlight touches them. False heather, a plant with numerous yellow, five-petaled flowers and scalelike leaves, survives because the leaves are scaly and thick and have very few stomata.

Other plants also grow on dunes, but in more protected places. Some of the most common are beach plums (which make great jams), beach heather, sea oats, yaupon, and seaside goldenrod. All must have ways of coping with the harsh environment of the sand dunes.

Plants which have leaves, roots or other parts modified for dry places are called **xerophytes.** (*Xero* means dry. *Phyte* means plant.)

Though some plants grow on them, dunes, unlike the vast majority of small worlds, do not have a web of life based on a rich supply of plants. Quite the opposite. Dunes therefore have remarkably few **herbivores**—that is, animals that live by eating plants. Most animals of the dunes are **carnivores.** Most animals, and especially the insects, eat insects. Most of the insects eaten have flown in from other areas. If there is any small world made up mostly of the hunters and the hunted, it is the dunes.

Very few animals spend their entire lives on sand dunes. It is too hot in the summer, too raw and cold in the winter, too dry and too windy. Like the plants, animals have great difficulty surviving on the dunes. Even so, a few manage it because they have made adjustments and adapted.

One insect found on most dunes is the black-and-yellow digger wasp, scientifically called the bembicid wasp. It is often seen hovering about a foot above the sand. It will suddenly drop to the sand, start digging in it, and after digging a while, will rise again into the air and hover. It is an odd way to act, but there is an explanation. The wasps do not have hairs to protect them from the heat. Because they can easily become overheated and die, they can dig in the hot sand only for a brief time. Every few minutes they rise up into cooler air, about a foot off the ground. The air even a foot above the sand is about 10° F. cooler than the sand.

A digger wasp digs a small tunnel into the sand so that

eggs can be laid in it. Once the tunnel is deep enough in the sand to be shaded, the wasp can enter it and stay cool. It no longer needs to hover in the air. When the tunnel is long enough, the female wasp will lay her eggs at the end of it.

A digger wasp

All insects on dunes have problems with the hot sands. This is especially true of the crawling insects, which either do not fly or fly rarely. They can, and most frequently do, dig down into the sand during the day and wait until night falls. Once the sands cool, they emerge and begin crawling about in search of food. Another way to escape the heat is to keep in the shade of plants, notably the dusty millers. Insects often crawl up the long grass stems of the marram grass to get into a cooler zone of air. At the same time, they might pick up breezes, often from the ocean, which cool them. During the day insects go higher on stems as the heat rises. As the air cools in the afternoon, they go lower on the stems.

Whitish-gray grasshoppers live on the sand, their white

color reflecting heat away from them. To cool off, these insects often stand high on their long legs to catch a slight breeze and to keep their bodies from touching the sand.

The most impressive hunting insect seen on the dunes is the cow killer. Folklore says that these bright red-and-black insects, which look like ants, have a sting that can kill a cow. Beware of them! In spite of appearances, these insects are not ants but wingless wasps.

Cow killers can go out on the roasting hot sands on days that would stop other insects. Their hairy bodies protect them from the sun, shading and insulating them from the heat though cow killers must seek shade when the temperature of the sand reaches 120° F.

A cow killer

Among the insects, as in all small worlds on land, there are those that feed on plants and those that hunt. Among most hunting insects of the world, only a few hunt large numbers of plant-eating insects. On the dunes we find an odd exception to this rule. On the dunes plant life and consequently plant eaters are scarce, so insect hunters must spend almost all their time hunting only other insect hunters.

Cow killers prey on weaker insects. Unlike the males,

female cow killers have wings. Since these red-and-black insects can fly, they search out digger wasp nests. They enter then and lay their eggs in digger wasp larvae. Once the cow killer eggs hatch, they eat the larvae. In addition, some types of bee flies parasitize cow killers, killing them. On the other hand, cow killers and robber flies will catch bee flies. But in the end digger wasps may kill and carry off bee or robber flies and put them in their nests so that their larvae may eat them. In a more or less circular fashion, the insects of the dune spend their time eating each other. This circle of death is highly unusual. Predators rarely live by mainly eating each other in such a fashion.

Of course, every now and then these hunting insects must also eat those insects that only eat plants. If they never ate plant-eating insects, they'd slowly die away for lack of nourishment. Because the dunes are so devoid of life, however, there are few plant-eating insects around. Most of the time the hunters are forced to eat only each other.

Various birds, which do not necessarily live on the dunes and certainly do not find water on them, fly over the dunes searching for insects. Among them are land birds, such as myrtle warblers and yellowthroats. A bird that lives on the dunes is the savannah sparrow. This is not an easy bird to identify. It is a small sparrow with a notched tail, pale eye stripes, and a dash of yellow in front of each eye. Its song is *tsip, tsip, tsip see, say.* Oddly enough, it sings on the ground. Half the food it eats consists of insects, the other half seeds.

Many seabirds, such as gulls and terns, and shorebirds like sandpipers and plovers, might be seen flying over dunes, but they have no real relationship with the dunes.

One of the few shorebirds to use the dunes is the oyster catcher. This is the only shorebird with a black head and a heavy red bill. Oyster catchers lay eggs on the sand dunes. They do not even make nests but leave their eggs to incubate in mere hollows. They probably use the dunes for egg laying because of the absence of animals that might search for eggs, such as rats, snakes, raccoons, and others. For egg laying the lifelessness of the dunes is a great advantage. As one might guess, the eggs are the color of the sand and hard to find.

Another animal that seeks out insects of the dunes is the toad. It is easy to confuse frogs and toads. Frogs have thin, often slimy skin and stay in or near water. Toads, however, have thick, waterproof skins and therefore can withstand the dry dunes. Unless you go out on dunes at night, you probably will not see any toads. Toads, like some insects, dig themselves into the loose sand during the day and remain cool and protected. At night they easily dig themselves out and go hunting for insects. The most common toad of the dunes is the Fowler's toad. It is much like the common toad, but its skin is less rough and it has a larger head.

One dune animal connected directly with the plants is the mouse. Mice eat the seeds from grasses and berries and fruits of dune plants. In spite of the fact that dunes are mostly bare sand, there are usually more than enough seeds, berries, and nuts around to feed numerous mice. The mice dig tunnels in the sand, usually under the matted roots of plants. During the day they hide there, keeping cool, until night falls. At night, they too roam the dunes in search of seeds, nuts, and, these days, litter.

The presence of the mice brings owls to the dunes. The

owls do not live there, though they might roost in pine trees. Quite a number of animals use the partly buried pine trees. The owls fly very silently and low over the sands listening for mice. Because a mouse out on the barren sands has almost no chance of escaping an owl, it is a good place for owls to hunt.

Some buried pines die. A short, stubby dead stem may stand above the sand. Rains falling on the stem cause it to rot as water oozes down inside the wood and along and under the bark hidden under the sand. Such pines will harbor colonies of termites that make numerous chambers in the rotting wood. Various types of beetles, too, can be found in the wood. Not infrequently mushrooms will grow on the damp stems.

One will not find mushrooms or termites on the living pines, but one can, at times, find various beetles (different from those of the wet, rotting wood) and other insects.

So far we have mentioned only the harsh aspects of the dunes and the life-and-death struggles of plants and animals—but we must not overdo this view. As in all small worlds, the dunes offer many advantages to the plants and animals that live there. In many ways, the dunes are the best place for them.

For one thing, dune plants are less disturbed by animals than plants in fields and forests. Dune plants will not be crushed by cow hooves or eaten by cows or deer or bears or most other large herbivores. Rarely will predators roam out on the lonely dunes to hunt the mice. All the flowers of the dunes need lots of sun and can be assured of receiving it there. Perhaps best of all for them, they do not compete with hundreds of other species of plants or contend with overcrowding. The same holds true for dune animals.

All the plants and animals of the dunes have built-in protection from the rigors of life. Through a long evolutionary process, they have been changed in form and structure to withstand dune living conditions. You might say that evolution designed them so that dune life would be the easiest possible life for them. Actually, most dune plants and animals could never live anyplace else.

When the science of ecology had just began, dunes were one of the first environments to be studied. In 1899 Professor Henry S. Cowles published a seminal paper about sand dunes, "The Ecological Relations of the Vegetation on the Sand Dunes of Lake Michigan." In this paper he pointed out that life on sand dunes goes through a succession of phases.

A sand dune starts out as a shifting world, hot, barren, and mostly lacking life. Eventually, however, all old dunes in temperate climates, where there is enough rainfall, become overgrown with plants: first the grasses, then such plants as beach heather, poison ivy, lupines, and dusty millers. These are followed by goldenrods and pitch pines. After many decades, maples, birches, or other broad-leaved trees grow there. The dunes then become one with the rest of the land. They are no longer dunes at all. They've become other hills in the landscape.

·3·

The World of the Milkweed

Of all the really interesting small worlds that one can easily find, that of the milkweed plant is probably the smallest.

You probably already know milkweeds. Their tufted seeds move by the tens of thousands on the winds of October and early November. As cool weather arrives, milkweed seed pods break open. Out of each one fly from one to two hundred seeds. Perhaps, too, you have touched the tufts and realized how fine, silky, and smooth they feel. One seed will have about nine hundred silky tufts on it.

Though milkweeds lend a touch of glory to autumn, they have of course existed all summer. The place to find and identify them is in open fields, vacant lots, and roadsides, most often in dry soils. Most prefer old meadows or roadsides. It is difficult to walk very far in such places without seeing a common milkweed *(Asclepias syriaca)*. In fact it would be difficult for you to miss this striking-looking tall weed. Clusters of showy pink and white flowers grow on it in June and July. It grows, at times, to a height of about three feet, sometimes five feet.

The individual flowers found in the clusters are one of the most unusual in the plant kingdom. The flower has five petals that are bent backward and downward. Above each bent petal is a nectar cup formed of five parts. In the cup are five hornlike projections. No other flower looks like it. Its odd shape and petals bent back and downward identify it. If you break off the stem of a milkweed, it will ooze with a milky, thick sap. The plant gets its name from the sap.

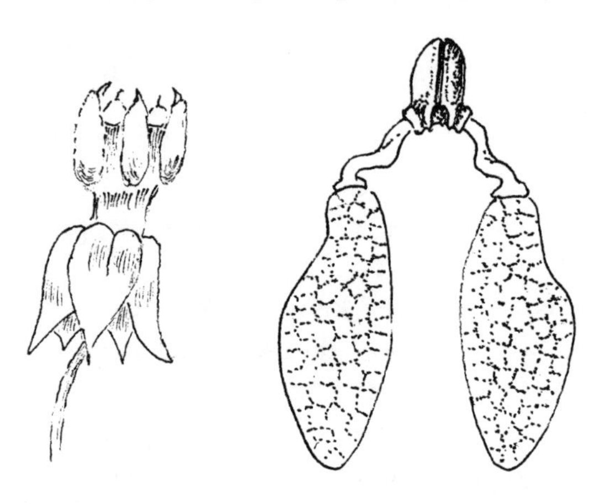

A milkweed flower and pollinium

Milkweeds often grow in fields that also have redtop grass in them. This grass, which is delicate looking and has a pinkish or reddish top, aids the milkweeds. The roots of redtop grass often form thick mats that keep out larger plants such as bushes and trees. In other words, they keep fields from becoming forests or shrubby areas. All this helps the milkweeds because they need to grow in open fields in the sun. Milkweeds do best where cold winter winds blow. The lack of trees in a field allows the wind to move freely. Milkweeds need a good long winter's dormancy.

A milkweed plant is a small world when it blooms. Many

types of insects gather around and on milkweed flowers. Literally dozens of species of insects may visit the flowers of a single plant. Some hover in the air near the plant. Others land on the flowers. Frequent visitors include butterflies and bees. If one carefully investigates the plants, one is likely to see many difficult-to-find insects clinging to stalks and leaves.

What is it that all these insects want? Why do they visit the milkweed at all?

Drawn to flowers by their colorful masses and fragrance, insects such as butterflies and bees come to the flowers to feed on the plentiful nectar, which is syrupy and sweet tasting. It is so thick and sweet that some Canadians boil milkweed flowers and obtain a brown sugar from them. The nectar of the milkweed flower (and of other flowers) is the only food these insects ever eat. Since milkweeds have many, many small flowers growing in large clusters, the insects can easily find nectar by visiting them. For a single plant it is a marvelous feeding place. Among the feeders one will almost always find bumblebees and honeybees. The honey made from milkweed nectar is delicious.

Though the insects need the milkweeds for nectar, the milkweeds, in turn, need insects for pollination. The flowers produce not only nectar, but **pollen** as well. Pollen, which looks like dust, contains the male cells of flowers. When the pollen from one flower comes in contact with the female ovules of another flower, the ovules become fertile, swell, and develop into seeds.

Unlike some flowers, those of the milkweed cannot send pollen away in the wind to other flowers. Milkweeds send their pollen to other milkweed flowers by means of insects. While feeding, insects, especially bees, get their feet caught in what is called a pollinium, a Y-shaped bag containing pollen. Once the pollinium has been caught on an insect's foot, the insect will carry it to distant flowers. When the insect lands on the new flower, the pollinium will get caught again and slip off the foot. Once in place in a new flower, the bag will dissolve. Long, hair-thin tubes from the pollen grains will seek the ovules there and fertilize them.

The complex structure of the pollinium and its ability to be trapped and carry out its mission to fertilize distant flowers is unique. In many ways it represents an extraordinarily close relationship between animals and plants. In no other small world can a more intimate plant-animal relationship be found. The foot trap, the slippery flower surfaces that force the insect's foot into the trap, the shape of the pollinium and its ability to rotate, once pulled away, so as to firmly grasp the leg, its capacity to be released at another flower and dissolve—the whole procedure is almost miraculous. It has developed over millions of years through a slow evolutionary process.

Although the transfer of pollen by insects is the only way to fertilization, there is another means by which milkweeds can reproduce themselves. New milkweed plants often sprout from the weed's extensive root system. A whole field of milkweed plants may have grown from a single root system. Though the plants may look like separate plants, they are in fact all connected by the huge root system. These plants are clones, each individual being identical to the other, whereas those milkweeds that develop from fertilized seeds are not alike. Each individual is in some small way different from all others.

There is a marvelous give-and-take between the milkweed flowers and their insect visitors. In this small ecosystem there is a major interaction between the milkweed plants and insects. It goes beyond the usual plant/animal relationship that calls for only a food chain, in which some animals eat the plants and give nothing to the plants in return.

The relationship between milkweeds and some insects does not stop there. Take the case of the monarch butterfly, which is often called the milkweed butterfly because of its close association with milkweeds.

The monarch is a common and very beautiful butterfly. Its wings are pumpkin-colored, with black veins and white spots. The monarch butterfly carries in its system an extraordinary chemical, a vile-tasting poison that can make birds sick. Any bird that snaps at a monarch will not do so twice. One experience with the vile chemical and ensuing sickness will be a lesson well learned.

The monarch butterfly does not manufacture the poison in its system but obtains it from milkweeds. And the butterfly obtains it while still a larva. To understand what a larva is we must take a brief look at the life cycle of a monarch butterfly. When a female lays her eggs—usually about four hundred of them, usually on milkweed plants, and, oddly enough, one egg to a leaf—the tiny pinhead-sized greenish-colored eggs hatch into larvae. These are more often called caterpillars. They eat the juices of the milkweed and absorb the poison, which is, chemically speaking, an alkaloid. (Common alkaloids are nicotine, found in cigarettes, and caffeine, found in coffee. Most taste bitter and many are poisons.) Once in the system of the caterpillar it will not leave it, even when the caterpillar later becomes an adult butterfly.

The poison protects the caterpillars from birds. If birds

do not attack the butterflies, one might wonder why the earth is not covered with monarch butterflies. Virus infections help keep their numbers down. Sometimes virus infections kill off whole populations of monarch butterflies. In huge areas of the country one might not find a single butterfly after such an epidemic.

Before becoming a butterfly, the green-black-and-white striped caterpillar must go through another stage of life. Once a larva reaches a mature age it builds a cocoon around itself. The cocoon of a monarch butterfly is like a jewel and is one of the most beautiful natural objects one can see. While inside its cocoon, the larva changes and develops a completely different type of body. It becomes a winged butterfly. Once the cocoon is broken open, the monarch butterfly, with poison in its system, flies away.

It is a highly unusual relationship, that between the monarch butterfly and the milkweed plant.

Monarchs are capable of migrating long distances, from Mexico and the California coast to Canada and back, but in speaking of monarchs we must use the term "migrate" carefully. It does not mean that individual monarch butterflies make the journey. In fact, very few, if any, go from the south to the north and return. What happens is that all go north in the spring. Along the way new generations appear, and those that were once in the south mostly die off. Those that reach the north turn around and fly south. Those going south have never been there before, yet, oddly, they know where to go, even finding special roosting trees along the way. Very lightweight tags placed on butterfly wings in Ontario, Canada, have been found in central Mexico 1800 miles south.

Viceroy butterflies may also show up at milkweeds. They

look almost exactly like monarchs, so much so that birds leave them alone. They evolved their look-alike appearances over millions of years and are now protected from birds.

In late summer one can usually find very bristly hairy caterpillars on milkweeds in the Northeast. These black-white-and-brown caterpillars are the larvae of the milkweed tiger moths. They feed almost exclusively on milkweeds and during the winter their cocoons can be found on milkweed stalks. Compared to the striking-looking caterpillar, the adult moth is a disappointing dull gray color, with a wingspan of an inch or sometimes two inches.

Sometimes moths called hummingbird moths feed during the day on milkweeds. These are big moths, with wingspans of about two and a half inches. Their wings lack scales in places, and so have see-through "windows" on them. But of greatest interest is their flight. They hover next to flowers just like hummingbirds while they sip nectar. It is easy to mistake them at first for hummingbirds.

When night falls and darkness comes, insects continue to visit the milkweeds. Noctuid moths, small moths with orange-brown forewings, sip nectar and so do geometrid moths, which are rather like them in looks but are larger and their forewings more yellow-orange and paler in color. Giant moths, the hawkmoths, also visit the milkweeds at night. Night and day, the sweet nectar feeds a host of insects.

Because so many insects fly to milkweeds, it is not surprising that some predatory insects hide in milkweed clusters so that they can attack. Among those that hunt for insects are the robber flies. They fly back and forth on patrol in front of milkweed plants. When an insect, even one much larger, comes in view, the robber fly attacks it, takes it to the ground, and makes a meal of it.

Waiting inside the flowers are small spiders called crab spiders. They do not build webs but depend on speed and powerful legs to grab insects. They are pale in color, like the flowers, and can easily hide. They are helped, too, by the fact that they have flat bodies. When these flower-colored spiders lie in wait, few insects can see them. One that gets too close will be grabbed by the spider's strong legs, held, and soon eaten.

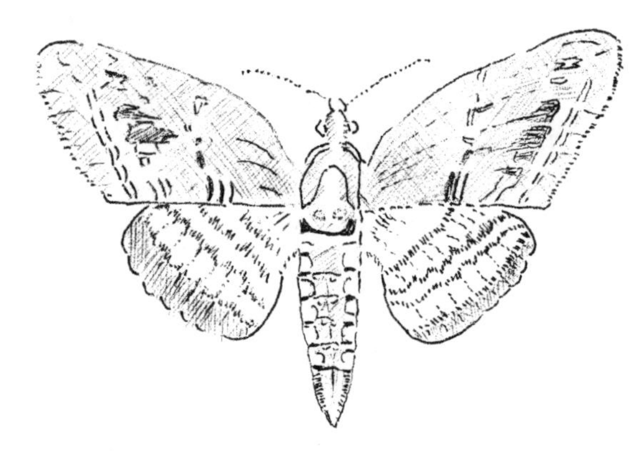

A hawkmoth

Funnel web spiders make funnel-shaped webs in among the flowers and leaves of milkweeds. They also catch many insects that visit the flowers and plants. You can identify the small funnel web spider because it appears to have ten legs. Actually it only has eight legs. The two "back legs" are not legs but spinnerets. Silk for their webs comes from them.

Though the flower cluster looks so beautiful to us, it is in a sense a ruthless world where the hunted and the hunters meet. But not all insects on milkweeds are one or the other. Aphids, for example, are strange little insects that eat plants and exude a sweet-tasting liquid. Carpenter ants love this liquid and often lick it off the aphids. Odd as it may seem, carpenter ants often herd aphids around, the way cowboys herd cattle. Like cowboys guarding cattle, the ants attack any other insects that might injure the aphids. Being strong and having powerful jaws that can inflict a

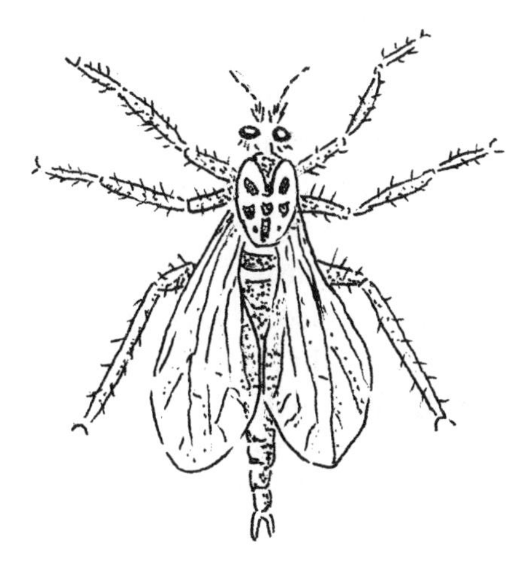

A robber fly

hard bite, the ants can well ward off most attackers. Most milkweeds harbor aphid "herds" and guardian carpenter ants.

It should be mentioned that aphids have a highly unusual life cycle. When aphid eggs hatch in the spring, only female aphids appear. Lacking any males they reproduce asexually. New generations of female aphids appear until autumn comes. When the autumntime eggs are laid, males finally hatch. They mate with females, who lay eggs in cracks in bark. In the spring the eggs hatch only females, and the cycle begins again.

Milkweed bugs also live on milkweeds. They are red and black in color and have a wide black stripe in the middle part of the body, with red markings on either side of it. In the fall, when milkweed pods develop, seeds grow larger inside them. Milkweed bugs get into the pods, puncture the seeds, place a tubelike mouth into the seeds, and pump saliva into them. The saliva dissolves the pulp of the seed and the bug sucks up the liquid pulp and in that way feeds itself. Sometimes unusually large numbers of these bugs kill so many seeds that there are many fewer milkweeds in the next generation of plants. Milkweed bugs, unlike the bees that carry away pollen, do no good to the milkweeds. They eat and give nothing in return.

Birds will also eat the seeds. One species of bird especially goes for them, and that is the lovely little black-gold-and-white goldfinch. The male goldfinch is mostly gold in color and has a little black cap on its head.

Milkweed bugs (*Oncopeltus fasciatus*) are small orange-red beetles with black dots on them. They live on the plants. Sometimes much larger insects, beetles with brilliant red bodies, also with black dots, may be found on milkweeds. They have long antennae. The scientific name for these beautiful creatures is *Tetraopes tetraophthalmus*. This name in English would indicate that the beetle has four eyes. Actually it has only two eyes, but each one is so divided that it appears to be two.

So it is that a milkweed, though a single plant far smaller than most trees, is in itself a small world having a population of insects, some of which must live there and no place else in this wide world.

·4·

A Tidal Pool

There is a strange beauty to most sea creatures. Gorgeous seashells, brilliantly colored fish, flowerlike sea anemones, richly colored sea urchins, and many others inhabit our shores. In addition unusual seaweeds cling to rocks to move and wave gracefully in the waves. Some appear as delicate as lace, others as green as green apples.

Unfortunately, if you walk along a wharf or stroll on a beach you will not see much, if any, of the beautiful life of the sea. In terms of seeing sea creatures, such walks often turn out to be disappointing.

The best way, and often the only way, to see the plants and creatures of the sea, without actually diving under the waves, is to find tidal pools. Tidal pools lie inside of natural basins that are formed in rocks along seashores. When the tide is high, waves and sometimes deep water cover the basins. When the tide goes out, the basins remain filled with water and isolated above the waves. All around them lies exposed land. Because tidal pools are always filled with water, they have sea creatures in them no matter what the tides.

No tidal pool is self-sufficient. All need to be replenished with the high tides. Even so, for several hours each day,

ish brown to green to blue-green, rich purple, and even red.

Worms and other tiny creatures can often live on seaweeds. Many larger animals, such as crabs and fish, hide behind floating seaweeds. In fact, some thick seaweed beds are small worlds in themselves.

In addition to the seaweed, there are many one-celled plants in the sea. Among them are dinoflagellates, which swim about in the water with small tails. There are other types of one-celled plants, too small to be seen with the naked eye, that drift on the surface of the sea. Mixed in with these one-celled plants live one-celled animals; together they are called plankton. When drifting plankton gets near shores, waves break and mix it into deeper waters. Small shrimp, clams, mussels, barnacles, and many other sea and tidal pool creatures eat plankton.

Thanks to the seaweeds growing on rocks and the plankton-filled water, a wide variety of animals can have a good food supply in a tidal pool.

The largest and most noticeable creature is the sea anemone, found in tidal pools along both the Atlantic and Pacific coasts of North America and in tidal pools and oceans all over the world. A person seeing a sea anemone for the first time will probably think that it is a flower. The top of it does have what appear to be petals open around it. The "petals" are not petals at all, however, but tentacles. When a sea anemone is hungry the tentacles stretch out, searching for a meal, constantly moving and feeling the water for food. Once the tentacles feel something such as a fish, some flesh, some scraps from a crab's meal, or similar food, they close on it and pull it into the round interior between the tentacles. This round hollow is actually the stomach of the sea anemone. There the creature digests the food and ejects the remains upward from its stomach. Sea anemones have hundreds of poisonous stingers. Their poison can stun an animal such as a fish and paralyze it.

Sea anemones often reproduce themselves by splitting in half. The upper half develops into a new sea anemone that looks like a jellyfish. Once developed, it drifts upward, leaving the original half below. Sea anemones can also reproduce themselves with eggs and sperm. Vast numbers of them may be released into the water and float away. When a floating egg is touched by a sperm, it becomes fertilized and a new sea anemone will start growing. Oddly, a sea anemone may hold fertilized eggs and larvae inside itself and later release as many as several hundred developed anemones at one time. This is a form of primitive parental care, for the sea anemones protect their young this way.

Some tidal pools are packed with sea anemones, many touching each other. Whole carpets of them can sometimes be found. Most are green, but some are white and others red. They often are highly colorful.

When the tide is high or when the sea anemones are under water in a tidal pool their tentacles usually remain open. If the tide is out and the sea anemones stand exposed to dry air, they will shut down and close their mouths and wait until the next tide. Thus, they conserve water and will not dry out. Once closed up, all their beauty is gone; they resemble soggy bags.

Sea anemones, in spite of appearances, do not remain stationary all their lives. That is not true. They can, and often do, move slowly about, going from one place to another.

It is a rare tidal pool that does not have crabs scurrying

about. They often crawl out of one tidal pool, cross dry rocks, and enter another. Crabs live a dual life. Much of the time they hunt prey, but at other times they are running or hiding from hunters. They are a good example of an animal in the middle of a food chain, being both a hunter and hunted.

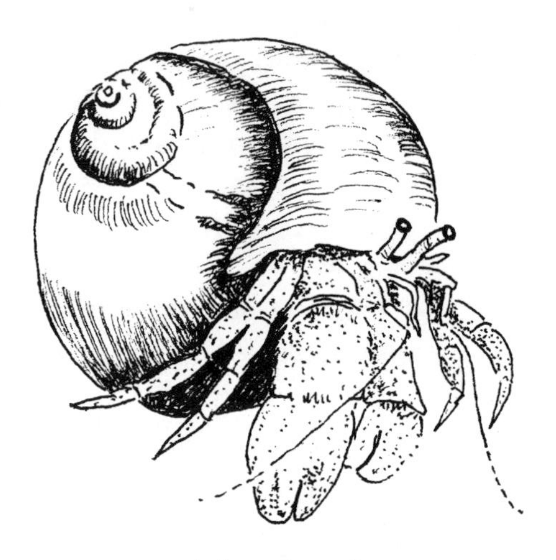

A hermit crab

Their way of life makes them wary. Much of the time they are looking this way and that with their eyes, which are on stalks. If they see prey or danger, they run quickly over the rocks or into crevices. Different species of crabs—and there are many species—eat different foods. Some eat seaweeds, others eat fish or shrimp, while others mainly scavenge and eat the remains of animals left by sea gulls.

In tidal pools one frequently sees purple-shelled mussels attached to rocks and sometimes to each other. In many places hundreds, even thousands of them cover the rocks.

When water covers a mussel it opens its shell, so that it can feed. Muscles in its body pump water through tubes. The mussel filters plankton and other microscopic plant and animal food particles out of the water. These stick to mucous membranes, where the mussel digests them.

If danger is about, mussels shut their shells. If you see a mussel with its shell open, touch it, and it will quickly slam its shell shut. Mussels also shut their shells to keep seawater inside during times of low tides, when they will be left high and dry for a few hours.

Mussels reproduce themselves by sending sperm and eggs into the water. Mussels can release over 60,000,000 eggs and countless sperm in one season. Most eggs remain unfertilized. Those eggs that are fertilized hatch small creatures that look nothing at all like adult mussels. These larvae resemble toy tops. For a while they drift about in the water, many being eaten by other animals. Eventually the larvae grow shells and then drop to the bottom of the pool. After a while, they touch down on a rock or sometimes on top of other mussels and exude from their shells stringlike objects called byssuses. These attach the mussels, by means of a superpowerful glue, to the rocks or to another mussel. Once held in place, mussels rarely move away, but they do wander. By exuding more strings and cutting away old strings with the sharp edges of their own shells, they can slowly but surely pull themselves along over the rocks.

The barnacle is another animal that can be found in all tidal pools. Most barnacles are white-shelled animals, which cling tightly to rocks. Many types look like tiny volcanoes, for they are somewhat cone-shaped and have a "crater" at the top. Oddly enough, in spite of their looks and stationary life, barnacles are actually related to shrimp. If you carefully opened up a barnacle and looked inside its shell, you would see a shrimplike animal.

When a barnacle feeds, little feelers reach out of the hole at the top of the shell, sweep the water, and pick up particles of food that are mostly too small to be seen with the unaided eye, and sweep the food into the shell.

Because barnacles remain attached to rocks for their whole lives, it is, of course, impossible for them to mate. Each individual barnacle solves the problem of reproducing itself by being two sexes at once—that is, a **hermaphrodite.** A single barnacle can produce both the eggs and the sperm needed to fertilize them. Like mussels, they release eggs and sperm into the water. A single barnacle can produce over a thousand eggs a year.

When the eggs hatch, young called nauplii appear, looking vaguely like very tiny shrimp and swimming about much the way shrimp do. After swimming out at sea for about three months, the barnacles come to shore, settle down on a rock, glue themselves to it for life, and within a day grow a shell around themselves.

It is easy to identify sea urchins. They look like round pincushions, with pins sticking out of them. Of course, these are not pins but spines. Beware of the spines. Some urchins have a few blunt spines; most have rather sharp ones. A few in tropical seas, and on Florida coasts, have sharp and very dangerous spines. They vary in color, but most are purple.

Sea urchins walk on dozens of tiny feet, moving about in an unusual manner. They fill some feet with water so that the feet expand. At the same time, they take water out of other feet, which collapse. As some are inflated, and others are deflated, the sea urchin is pushed along. (Starfish, which are very closely related to sea urchins, move in exactly the same manner.) Though they cannot go fast, they must move about, going from one place to another in their endless search for food. They can feed on plants, barnacles, and at times even mussels. A sea urchin has its mouth oddly placed, at the center of the underside of its body. The mouth can grind up food, even tough barnacles, with very powerful mill-like structures.

What would the seashore be without starfish? Without doubt this is the best known seacoast animal of all. Starfish are voracious hunters. They attack oysters and mussels, prying them open with their powerful bodies. Once a starfish gets a shell open, it extrudes its stomach, puts it into a crack between the two shells, and actually wraps it around an oyster or mussel. Once in the lining of the stomach, a mussel or oyster is digested.

As tides go down, fish sometimes become isolated in tidal pools and must stay there until the next high tide releases them. One such fish is the goby, a small fish with many fins. Gobies often stay near the bottom of tidal pools, almost invisible because of their coloration and small size, grabbing tiny marine worms or other small animals. They are amazing fish, for they can actually walk across the rocks using their fins. Sometimes they will travel from one tidal pool to another; sometimes they will go back into the waves and swim free into the ocean.

Other small fish that live near rocky shores may get caught in tidal pools—sculpins, for instance, which have broad heads, thin bodies, and large fanlike fins. Most people would find them exceptionally ugly-looking fish. Also caught often in tidal pools are cunners, common fish found around most piers and rocky shores. They have large scales and a continuous row of fins on their back. Their mouths are small and they have thick lips. Tautogs are much like cunners in appearance. They are gray and black, or just black, so black that another name for the tautog is blackfish.

Sponges often grow in tidal pools along the northern Atlantic and Pacific oceans. Unlike bath sponges, American sponges of our northern shores are not large or dramatic. In fact, they cannot be used as bath sponges because inside of them are slivers of calcified "glass."

Sponges look as though they do nothing at all. No animal looks so inactive. Yet in truth sponges are very active, for they must pump great amounts of water throughout their breadth and length. During its lifetime a sponge might pump thousands of gallons of seawater through the thousands of pores inside of it. It has been calculated that a sponge about the size of an apple will pump twenty-five gallons a day. As the water is pumped through, small tentacles, like microscopic feelers, inside of tubes, take food from the water and digest it. In actuality a sponge is made up of hundreds of separate animals joined together. Sponges come in various shapes. In still water, a sulfur sponge, which is bright yellow, may have branches, but where the surf hits it, it will be flat and cling to the rocks.

Tunicates (often called sea squirts) look so much like sponges that one might mistake one for the other. Actually sea squirts are vase-shaped and have two distinct openings, much like the openings of many vases. In contrast sponges have *many* small openings. Sea squirts are found clinging to rocks in tidal pools. One who looks at them for the first time might come to the conclusion that they are primitive animals, as primitive, for example, as jellyfish or sponges. Oddly enough, they are far more closely related to you and me than to sponges. In spite of their looks sea squirts are highly evolved animals.

We can divide the animal kingdom into two groups. The primitive group lacks backbones. The higher group has backbones. Animals such as sponges, worms, jellyfish, and insects are primitive and lack backbones. More highly advanced animals, such as fish, reptiles, birds, and mammals all have backbones. So do the young tunicates. (The adults cross the line, however. As adults, tunicates are primitive animals, lacking a backbone.) Tunicates are on the fence that separates the primitive, lower animals from the higher animals. In that sense they rate as one of the world's most unusual animals.

Quite often, jellyfish manage to get trapped by the tides in tidal pools. In spite of their simple looks, jellyfish are, in many ways, fascinating animals. They have a visible nervous system. One can actually see it inside their transparent bodies. The nervous system is extraordinarily primitive. It only allows the jellyfish to swim by moving its muscles up and down, so that it swims in an odd waving motion. The thin tentacles that hang down from the underside of a jellyfish catch prey. The stingers contain poison that stuns small animals, such as tiny fish. (Beware of jellyfish. Some can give you terrible stings.) Jellyfish usually catch and devour fish but will also eat other animals.

If you imagine how a jellyfish would look upside down, you can see that it is related to a sea anemone. Both have circular rings of tentacles that have stingers. The mouth in both animals is found in the middle of a circle of tentacles.

Limpets are cone-shaped shellfish. They are related to

snails, but their shell is not coiled. Many limpet shells resemble coolie hats. Limpets eat the thin coatings of algae that grow on rocks. They often live in places where heavy surfs pound the rocks, but no surf could pull a limpet off a rock. Each limpet finds a place on the rocks for its permanent home. It can cut into the rock with its shell, and while the limpet grinds away, the rock will in turn file away the edge of the shell. Eventually the limpet shell will fit tightly against the rock, the fit so snug that during low tides exposed limpets can stay attached to the rock and preserve water inside their shells. When the tide is up, the limpet will graze a few feet away from its "home place" and eat algae. Just before the tide goes out, the limpet will return to its place and clamp itself to the rock again.

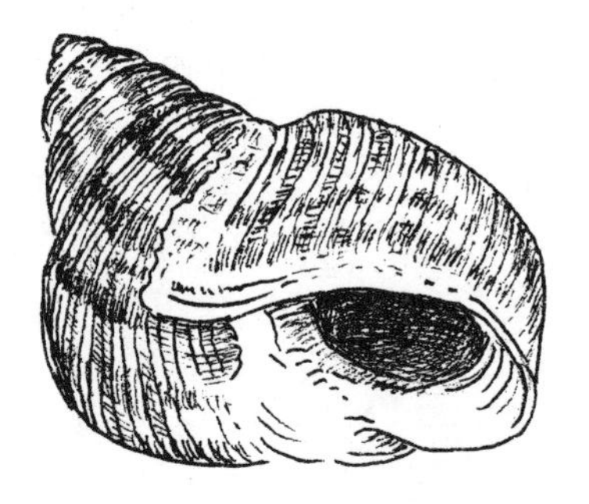

Periwinkles

Periwinkles are charming little snails. They "graze" about, eating small algae with their rasplike teeth, scraping them off rocks. There are three kinds of periwinkles. Each type grows in a different tidal zone. The rough-shelled periwinkles live only where highest tides occur. If they are in the water at all it is when spray from breaking waves is thrown over them. These periwinkles are really more land creatures than sea creatures. The most common type of periwinkles, which have brownish-colored shells, live in the zone between high tides and low tides. If they need to, they can survive for hours out of the water. The smooth-shelled periwinkles must always be covered with water, so they live below the lowest tides, or in tidal pools.

Periwinkles connect the world of the sea with the world of the land. Land snails evolved from sea snails. Some day, way off in the future, some type of periwinkle will probably be a land animal. All life on land started in the sea. One creature after another became adapted to life in tidal pools. Later, they lived on land when the tide was low. They lived on dry land for longer and longer periods of time: hours, days, weeks, months, years, then all the time. In short, they became land animals. So might some periwinkles.

·5·

The World of Cliffs and Boulders

Cliffs and boulders present plants and animals with many challenges. So great and remarkable are they that few plants and animals can overcome them. Some cliffs and boulders often remain barren of life for centuries. Others have some life on them but usually not much.

The very steepness of cliffs and boulders keeps away most life. Few animals could or would climb up a high cliff. The lack of soil and the weather keep away most plants. Because of their shape, cliffs influence the local weather. Winds hitting cliffs often gather speed. Updrafts and downdrafts swirl around them. Gales buffet them; lightning often hits the higher parts of cliffs. On sunny, calm days in summertime south-facing cliffs can be brutal places for life, much too hot for most plants. The temperature can climb to 150° F. on the rocks. On the other hand, ice might cling to frigid north-facing cliffs for months on end.

Worst of all, however, is the dryness. Rainwater simply bounces off cliffs and boulders and is immediately gone. For weeks, even months, there may be no water on cliffs.

In spite of all this, most places, even many of the steepest cliffs, do have life, and so do most boulders. Highly interesting life appears, even where least expected.

Lichens can, and usually do, grow on many cliffs and boulders, such as those made of granite, but they do not grow on all types of rock because lichens cannot stand the chemical composition of all stones. They do not, for example, grow on limestone. In addition, lichens will not grow where the air is polluted, especially with sulfur compounds. Wherever you find lichens you can be sure the air is clean and fresh.

Lichens are strange for, in spite of appearances, each lichen is composed of two plants. One is an alga and the other a fungus. The fungus part is tough and rather leathery in texture. The hard top of the fungus protects the plant from damage. The lower part of the fungus is able to grip sheer rock cliffs. It has rootlike **rhizoids** that can grip a rock very tightly. Lichens can grow on the steepest of cliffs. The rhizoids are not true roots. True roots absorb water and minerals, but the rhizoids do not; they merely hold the plants in place. They allow the lichens to grow on the steepest of cliffs on otherwise bare rock. Sometimes they even allow the lichens to grow upside down under overhangs.

The alga part of the lichen plant is succulent—that is to say, it can hold water in its cells. When rains come the alga part of the lichen obtains water and swells up. It stores it until it is needed. Most important, the algae contain chlorophyll. The chlorophyll gives most lichens their green color. It is also in red, yellow, and black lichens, but it is masked by other colors. Chlorophyll is a chemical that can convert sunlight, water, and carbon dioxide into oxygen and food, mainly sugars and starches. The chlorophyll found only in the alga part of the plant is capable of producing enough food not only for itself but also for the fungus.

Thus the alga and fungus cooperate beautifully. Such a helpful, cooperative system is called a **symbiosis.** Lichens are an example of one of the most successful of all such symbiotic relations to be found in nature.

There are a great many varieties of lichens. The most common is the ring lichen. It appears to grow in concentric circles, forming rings like those seen on a target. Ring lichens grow very, very slowly. Photographs taken of lichens on rocks on Isle Royale, Lake Superior, show no noticeable growth over a seventeen-year-period. Yet, the plants in both photographs were alive and thriving. Some are hundreds of years old. In the Arctic, where they grow even more slowly, some are at least a thousand years old. Old ring lichens are the oldest plants in the eastern part of America. In the West, only the bristlecone pines and sequoias outlive them.

Though ring lichens grow flat on the cliffs, a lichen called shield lichen resembles gray, fallen leaves, which appear stuck on the cliff. Rock tripe is another lichen that looks leafy. Mealy goblet lichens resemble little vases or goblets; they grow in the soil blown into cracks and ledges.

Many lichens are brightly colored. In fact, because of their colors, people have used them for centuries as dyes for woolens. They were originally used for colorful Scottish kilts. Some lichens found on cliffs are bright yellow, others a startling orange, others a rich black color. British soldier lichens are tipped with a brilliant red. (The British soldiers in the American Revolutionary war wore bright red uniforms. It is believed that the lichens received their names from them.) The British soldier lichens look like little twigs topped with red tips. They also grow in cracks and along ledges.

At some time in their history, new cliffs stand barren, exposed to the sun, wind, and rain. All that can be found on them are microscopic plants and bacteria. A new cliff might be formed after rocks have split off it and fallen away. A cliff might be exposed after a glacier has melted. Cliffs might be scoured clean by falling rocks in an avalanche. Obviously such newly formed cliffs are rarely seen.

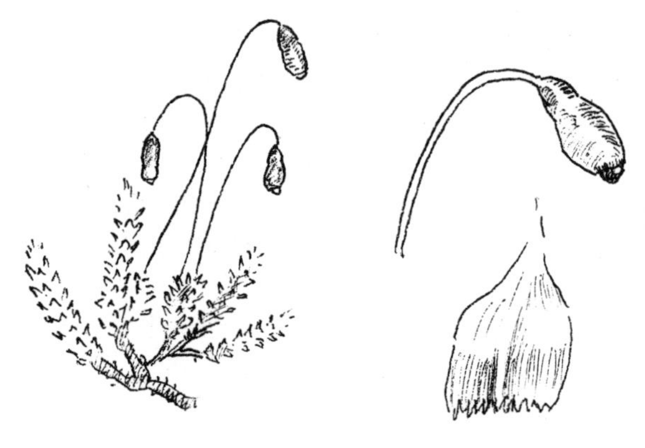

Silver moss

The first plants visible to the unaided eye to appear on cliffs are lichens. They are followed by mosses, primitive plants that, unlike higher plants, lack roots and stems. Mosses have "leaves," called **thalli** but unlike true leaves these lack veins. Mosses never grow large because they do not have tubes inside to carry food, water, and minerals. Only higher plants have such tubes. Lacking them, mosses must always be small.

The first mosses to appear on rocky cliffs and boulders are usually *Bryum* and *Grimmia.* One common type of *Bryum* is silver moss, so named because as the moss gets old, chlorophyll moves away from the tip of the leaves. These mosses in bright sunlight do look silvery and shiny.

Grimmia is a tufted moss that forms thick carpets, almost velvety in feel. The moss is very dark, almost black at times.

Other plants that can grow on sheer cliffs are spike mosses. Spike moss *Selaginella* form thick green carpets on rocks, for they crowd together so closely. The moss is gray-green and its leaflike thalli spiral around what appears to be a stem. Rock spike mosses never grow more than about three inches high.

Lichens and mosses tend to destroy a cliff—ever so slowly, of course. In a century one would not notice much destruction. Yet, as time goes on the lichens release a corrosive substance called carbonic acid. At the same the lichens' rhizoids wedge themselves into hairline cracks and pull out small grains of rock. So do the mosses. Little by little, century by century, millennium by millennium, the rock turns to soil.

Once soil is formed it blows into cracks and onto ledges of cliffs. All cliffs, even the steepest and smoothest-looking, have cracks and ledges on them. As the cracks become filled and packed with soil, rainwater will dampen the soil.

New types of plants other than lichens or mosses can start growing in the damp soil. Usually these plants are grasses. Broom sedge, which has tufted, feathery spikes, grows from about a foot to three feet high. Another grass found on cliffs is turkeyfoot. It often has a distinct top, usually with three spikes, which does resemble a bird's foot. It is a rather large grass, growing as high as six feet. There may also be bluejoint and beard grass.

Once grasses appear, ants will arrive. They can climb up any cliff, no matter how steep. They eat the seeds and whatever windblown foods they can get. The soil is necessary to the ants for they must build colonies in it.

A few wild flowers such as dwarf buttercups and bluets and wood sorrels grow on cliffs where there are dirt-filled cracks. Wood sorrels are lovely flowers. You can identify them easily for they have five pinkish or whitish petals and large leaves that look like clover leaves. On calm, windless days, butterflies might sip nectar from the wild flowers.

Following the grasses and a few wild flowers come the bushes. Bunchberries will start growing in cracks and on ledges. Bunchberries, closely related to dogwood trees, have what appear to be four large petals when in flower. Actually they are **bracts,** colored leaflike structures that will attract insects. Inside the four white bracts are tiny flowers. Eventually berries will appear.

Highbush blueberries will also grow in cracks and on ledges. Like bunchberries (which are quite tasteless), tasty blueberries attract birds and small mammals.

Finally, many, many decades—even centuries—after the first lichens have appeared on the cliffs, the **climax plants** appear. The climax plant species will be the last ever to appear. No new types of plants will ever replace them; they are the culmination of a long succession. Individual plants will, of course, die away, but those that replace them will be like the ones that died.

The climax plants usually are highbush blueberries and cranberries and the first real trees. Among these are eastern red cedar. This tree has small, soft, blue cones, often covered with a waxy substance. The tips of the needles are prickly. The bark is loose and often hangs down, long and fibrous. In swamps and damp forests the red cedars may grow very tall, to about fifty feet, but cliffs are difficult places to live, with winds, scorching sun, and cracks so small that the tree roots can never grow large. The red cedars on cliffs are dwarf trees. (It should be added in passing that Japanese bonsai trees are kept small by cramping their roots. The same thing happens naturally to many trees growing from cliff cracks.)

Another cliff tree is the balsam fir. The best way of identifying it is by the sweet, pungent smell of balsam. All firs have upright cones, and so do balsam firs. Old cones fall apart leaving a spike behind. Young trees have resin blisters on their bark. When the trees grow old, the bark becomes reddish in color. Balsam firs are amazingly limber. Winds cannot break them, for they bend this way and that as though made of rubber.

Staghorn sumac trees may also grow on cliffs. Their branches, when bare, do resemble the antlers of stags. The tips of the branches have velvety red-rust-colored masses of berries on them. The tips are distinct in shape, like long, thin footballs.

Gray birches also may be seen growing in cracks and on ledges. They have white bark, which looks like the bark on paper birch trees, but where the bark on paper birch trees peels off easily, that on gray birches does not peel away at all. Gray birches are the only birches to have triangular-shaped leaves.

The most marvelous thing about gray birches is their roots. Some snake and wiggle for long distances all over rocks and cliffs as they seek cracks and water. Sometimes they are weird looking and wonderful to see.

Few animals can climb high, steep cliffs or get onto the tops of boulders. Even so, there is animal life to be found on high, steep cliffs.

In addition to the ants, many spiders make their home on cliffs. They build webs across cracks and in the branches of trees and bushes. These webs catch passing insects. Spiders that live on cliffs do quite well because the winds near and around cliffs often blow this way and that. Confused insects frequently get blown by updrafts and downdrafts into these waiting spider webs. Others are caught as they come to visit wild flowers. Once caught, the insect will be killed and eaten by the spider.

Many will not get caught. Some moths may go unharmed to visit balsam firs. A few bees, butterflies, and other insects will visit wild flowers. Bark beetles and wood borers will invade the trees, both living and dead. Otherwise there is not much that would interest an insect.

As anyone who lives where snails are common will know, snails can easily crawl up a pane of glass. It is nothing at all for a snail, or its close relative, a slug, to climb up the steepest rock cliffs. They can eat vegetable debris, which is often on the rotten side, found under the plants. They find food by smell, and as they move about can look over obstacles with their eyes, which are on the tips of moveable stalks.

The blood of cold-blooded animals is about as cold as the surrounding air. When the temperature goes below freezing, one would think that the blood of a land snail should freeze. It does not. Snails will move about in rather cold weather. However, if it gets too cold they will bury themselves deep under leaves in places where rotting vegetation gives off some heat.

Harvestmen are often called daddy longlegs, and with good reason, for they have very long and very thin legs. They are not very closely related to most spiders. They belong to the order, Opiliones. Unlike other spiders, the head of a harvestman is attached not to the front of its body but to the top of it. On its head it has two largish eyes. Harvestmen mostly eat insects. Sometimes they may eat the flesh of dead animals or suck juices from plants, such as mosses.

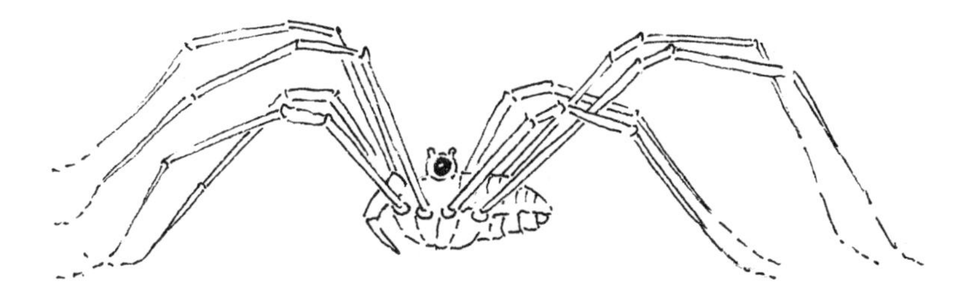

A harvestman (daddy longlegs)

Oddly enough, toads are found on the ledges of cliffs. They, like the spiders and harvestmen, are attracted by the insects. An average toad, it has been estimated, will eat about one thousand insects a year. A small valley with cliffs may easily have in it a thousand toads, which can eat a million insects a year.

In the West, rattlesnakes often spend much of their time on cliffs, on ledges, in crevices. Like all snakes they sun themselves when they are too cold and retreat into rock crevices when too hot. These activities warm or cool their blood, which does not naturally remain warm. This is why they are called cold-blooded animals. (All animals except for birds and mammals are cold-blooded.) A few rattlesnakes remain in the East, but they are extraordinarily rare, almost extinct.

Black snakes are large snakes that live on cliffs. They are black on top and whitish below. As hunters of mice, chipmunks, red squirrels, and birds, they are part of the **food chain** of the cliff world. This food chain is less developed in the world of cliffs than elsewhere because of the lack of rich plant life and because so few animals live on cliffs. Yet it is a food chain.

A food chain tells us who eats whom. All food chains begin with plants. Some plant will be eaten by some animal—say, an insect—which is eaten by a mouse, which is eaten by a hawk. So a food chain is a sequence of feeders.

Several types of large birds, such as hawks and vultures, seek out the updrafts that rise against the face of cliffs because these winds make it easier for them to gain altitude. Instead of wasting energy flying upward, they allow the updrafts to carry them to higher altitudes.

One of the best places to watch large hawks and vultures, and sometimes eagles and osprey, is on top of cliffs. The most common vultures seen near cliffs are turkey vultures. They have very large, long wings, often six feet in length, and are easy to identify because of their size, their red heads, and their unmistakable wings, which are black in front and white in back. Many hawks visit cliffs, the most common and most easily identified of which is the red-tailed hawk, the only one to have a red tail. Another easily identified hawk often seen near cliffs is the red-shouldered hawk, the only one with red shoulders and a black and white striped tail.

Though these vultures and hawks are part of the small world of cliffs, they really have no association with the life of the cliffs. They are not part of the "food chain" because they neither eat plants nor animals of the cliff, nor are they eaten by animals on the cliffs.

Some hawks, including rough-legged hawks, sparrow hawks, and duck hawks, do use the cliffs as nesting sites. These nests are often crude, nothing more than a collection of sticks and down on the rocks. Other birds that nest on cliffs are the common pigeon and the cliff swallow, which builds vase-shaped nests of mud having entrances at the bottom of the nests. They are attached to the side of the cliff, usually under overhangs. All these birds, and other species as well, benefit from the safety of the cliffs, which no foxes, weasels, or similar predators can climb.

Of all the birds that frequent cliffs, none is more interesting than the hummingbird. They do not come to the cliffs because of the rocks, updrafts, or to nest or feed. They visit cliffs, first of all, for nesting materials. Hummingbirds build small, thimble-sized nests, which are lined with lichens and mosses. They will fly long distances to pick up nesting materials from cliff sites and fly back to their nests carrying them in their bills.

Hummingbirds visit cliffs, too, in order to clean their feathers, as all birds must do so that they can fly. Most birds clean their feathers with their bills, but the bills of hummingbirds are much too long to reach all their feathers, so those that live close to cliffs often seek out places where trickles of water, sometimes even small waterfalls, course down a cliffside. The hummingbird gets into the stream of falling water, hangs onto mosses, and allows the water to pour over it, cleaning its feathers.

Hummingbirds are easy to identify. They are by far the smallest of birds and can, unlike other birds, fly backward or hover in one spot. Their long bills are very thin and needlelike.

One might wonder why hummingbirds would dare to come to cliffs often patrolled by hawks. The little birds have nothing to fear. First, no hawk could possibly catch a hummingbird on the wing. If a hawk dives at one, the hummingbird can easily dart backward or forward and get out of the way. Secondly, a hummingbird does not mind using its needlelike bill as a dagger. A few jabs with that bill will keep any hawk away, especially if it is jabbed in the eye.

There are many hummingbirds in western America; to identify them one would need a good bird book. But east of the Mississippi River there is only one: the ruby-throated hummingbird. And it does have a ruby throat.

Cliffs are much too steep for most mammals. Very, very few can or will climb up them. Various species of chipmunks might be seen on cliff ledges. So might red squirrels. One mammal that often lives on rocky cliffs is the white-footed mouse (genus *Peromyscus*). These mice in many, many ways are very different from the common mice found in houses. The white-footed mouse does have white feet and white legs and belly. The upper parts can vary in color from gray to golden brown. Unlike our house mice, white-footed mice are very clean and spend a great deal of time grooming themselves.

They sometimes make their nests in trees but often in rock crevices. Rock conducts heat very rapidly. This is why a stone feels colder to the hand than a piece of wood. The heat of your hand travels quickly into the rock. The mice living in crevices insulate the walls of their nests with thick layers of leaves, shredded bark, and similar materials. Their well-lined nests, protected from wind and rain, can be very cozy.

White-footed mice do not **hibernate** in the wintertime. They spend summers and autumns gathering and hiding seeds; during the worst of the winter, they survive on their stored seeds. They are fascinating little creatures that are a joy to watch.

A white-footed mouse

In the western parts of our country there lives a mammal called a pika, which never leaves the world of the cliffs. Distantly related to rabbits, they are small mammals, tail-less, the color of rocks, and therefore often difficult to see. Like white-footed mice, they do not hibernate, but gather food into a "haystack." Some haystacks of food are about 8⅛″ × 8⅛″ × 8⅛″, about a peck in size, a lot for such a small creature, only about seven inches long, to gather. A pika protects its food supply, even with its life.

Pikas live in cold places, often far above timberline. Few mammals live in such cold, far-off places. Mountain climbers know these little animals, for they sometime do rest and sun themselves, and most curious of all, they whistle. To our ears, in lonely places, it is a cheery sound, but it is really a call to other pikas.

Though lacking in variety and richness, the world of cliffs is truly different from all others. In many ways, it is strange, even alien.

·6·

An Old Wooden Barn

A barn usually includes a main room, grain rooms, and, high above, a hayloft. One can always find something going on with cows, chickens, and other animals. Birds fly in and out. Chickens cluck, pigeons coo, and occasionally a cow will moo good and loud. In old wooden barns one can discover nooks and crannies and dark mysterious corners and on windy days can hear the strange creaking sounds the barn makes.

A barn is a small world, a unique ecosystem set apart from all others. Unlike almost all other small worlds, it shelters both wild and domestic animals.

Farmers build barns for various purposes: to protect domestic animals and to store hay, feed, grains, and equipment, such as plows, saddles, and tools. In barns one can often find workrooms and sometimes bunk rooms for helpers.

In thinking of a barn as a small world, one would naturally start with the farmer's animals, which are usually cows, horses, chickens, and goats.

At night, and at times during the day, many barns shelter dairy cows. On most farms, the cows do not spend all their time in the barn. Dairy cows usually feed outdoors in pastures during the day. When it is time to be milked the cows will return to the barn. They do not need to be called into the barn, for the milk will swell in their udders and hurt them. They are milked twice a day.

There is no good reason why cows are milked inside a barn, aside from comfort for the person milking them, and protection of the cows from the weather. (If milking machines are used, as they are on large dairy farms, then the cows must be in the barn.) If cows stay out in too hot or too cold weather, they will use up energy staying either cool or warm. This means they will produce less milk. When they are placid and comfortable in a barn, their milk production goes up. The same holds true for goats.

In the summer, as cows and goats leave pastures for barns, they may bring with them various insects, sometimes ticks and other pests, which will spread to other animals in the barn and to humans as well. Such pests account for much of the "wild" life in a barn.

Horses are strong and hardy animals and can easily stay outdoors during a severe cold, windy winter. Most horses on western ranches, where temperatures can be 100°F. in the summer and −40°F. in the winter, never enter barns. Horses in other parts of the country do spend much of their time in barns, where they eat less.

If the barn houses valuable horses, a farmer will often keep a pony with a horse. The pony, which is a calm, placid animal, serves as a "friend" for the horse. Because the horse has its friend, it will not be so nervous or restless. A friendly relationship between animals is quite rare in any small world. (In higher animals in the wilds, such as among chimpanzees, dolphins, wolves, and coyotes, there are friendship patterns.) In this case, the relationship helps the horse and probably the pony as well. Their friendship makes life less stressful. Animals under stress are less likely to survive than those that are calm. Nervous animals may take up bad eating habits or get into dangerous fights. Diseases often spread more quickly in nervous animals than in calm ones. So, odd as it may seem at first, friendships among animals help them live longer.

Chickens, much more than cows, horses, or goats, need the protection of a barn, though if they must, they can survive outdoors on their own. This is so because compared to cows, horses, or goats, chickens are small animals that are sometimes killed by predators. Barns offer a good deal of safety against weasels, foxes, and other predators that on rare occasions kill the chickens. (Actually a very small percentage of chickens die because predators kill them. The vast majority die of diseases, by becoming overheated, and from other causes. All in all, predators do not make a dent in chicken populations.)

Most farm chickens will roost in separate rooms in barns overnight. They roost on high horizontal bars, where predators such as cats cannot get them while they sleep. If a dog lives in the barn, the chickens will be very safe. Like all animals, chickens eat less if protected in a barn.

During the day chickens can pretty well protect themselves in or out of the barn. It is a foolish cat that would mix with one. A chicken can be dangerous when it pecks an enemy. If a chicken sees a larger, more dangerous animal it can fly up to an overhead rafter or to the roost and escape it.

Farmers usually keep barn cats. These cats never become pets. Aside from providing them with water, the farmer leaves them alone and in that way encourages them to be wild animals. These cats, never fed by humans, must hunt to survive—and hunt they do. As we will soon see, there is plenty for them to hunt: mice, birds, and small predators. Cats will rarely, if ever, tackle such predators as foxes or large snakes. Even so, their presence in the barn will usually keep such predators away. Like all animals, predators desire an easy life. Though they realize they could kill a cat, it is a lot easier to avoid a fight and obtain food more peacefully someplace else. In terms of survival, it is better to get food the peaceful, easy way, for that takes less energy.

Some farmers own dogs that stay all the time in barns, but most dogs live a more varied life. They spend perhaps a third of their lives in the farmhouse, a third in the barn, and a third in the fields. A dog will defend a barn against intruders. Terriers are large enough to tackle rats and kill them. In fact, they make excellent ratters. Larger dogs will attack, but rarely manage to kill, foxes and snakes.

The farmer's animals attract a wide variety of insects to a barn. Female mosquitoes need the blood of birds and mammals, for blood allows their eggs to develop. If the female mosquito cannot find any such blood, its eggs will never hatch. (While female mosquitoes bite the domestic animals, the male mosquitoes, which never bite birds or mammals, are off someplace sipping flower nectar.) A barn offers a mosquito welcome shelter from the wind. Mosquitoes do not fly about outside when it is windy; they wait in bushes until calm weather returns. In a barn they can fly about at all times. Mosquitoes thrive in barns, too, because they are semidark, and mosquitoes hunt mostly at dusk and twilight. In the barn they find such dull lighting conditions all day long. Moreover, there are so many barn animals for them to bite, plus wild birds, rats, mice, and of course the farmer and workers.

A number of flies also bite animals and people, including the vicious black horseflies. These are large, sometimes a full inch in length. A bite from a horsefly is something a person will remember for a long time.

Stable flies look a great deal like houseflies. One way to identify them is to see how they rest. When a stable fly rests, it keeps its wings out and away from its body. A housefly does the opposite and keeps its wings next to its body.

A stable fly

Most flies that live in stables prefer to lay their eggs in horse dung. The dung stays warm as it rots so that the eggs can incubate. When the eggs hatch, maggots (the young larvae of the flies, which look like little grains of rice or tiny white worms,) crawl on and in the dung. Eventually, maggots change into adult flies.

Lice are a problem for animals, and occasionally for humans as well. Chickens, for example, often have lice in their feathers. Lice are very small insects, that look rather like little white worms, about one-fifth of an inch in length. Because of their size it is difficult to see one.

Some animals bring ticks in from the fields. These small but dangerous creatures are not insects. Unlike insects, which have six legs, ticks have eight legs. They have flat bodies. Dog ticks are about one-fifth of an inch long, brown in color with white markings. Some ticks transmit very dangerous, even deadly viral diseases. (Most people who get such diseases get them *not* in barns but on hikes outdoors.)

It might be added that many animals have worms and other parasites, but the average visitor to a barn would almost never see them.

Not only do animals attract insects but so do hay, grains, and other foods. One of the main purposes of a barn is to store hay. The roof and walls keeps hay dry and usable for months at a time. In the summer and autumn, farmers bring hay into barns from their hayfields. This hay always has many insects in it, as well as mice, perhaps a few snakes, even birds, and a few stray toads. Those animals that do not have any reason to be in a barn and that can escape will soon leave, but many insects brought into the barn will continue to live in the hay for a few weeks or months.

The hay will have in it and on it many insect eggs. These will hatch eventually and these insects will live in the barn at least for short periods of time and perhaps for months.

Farmers also buy grains (or raise their own) and store them in their barns. Corn, oats, wheat, and other types of grain often contain various species of flour beetles, such as many species of darkling beetles. Adult darkling beetles are large, powerful black beetles about an inch in length. The adults do not damage the grain, but the young larvae do. These are the mealworms that one buys to feed birds and small pets. At times mealworms can be serious pests. Many other beetles and moths attack grain.

For some, the most interesting thing about the hay, grain, and any other food in the barn is that it attracts large animals from the outside. A good many birds and rodents enter a barn because of that food.

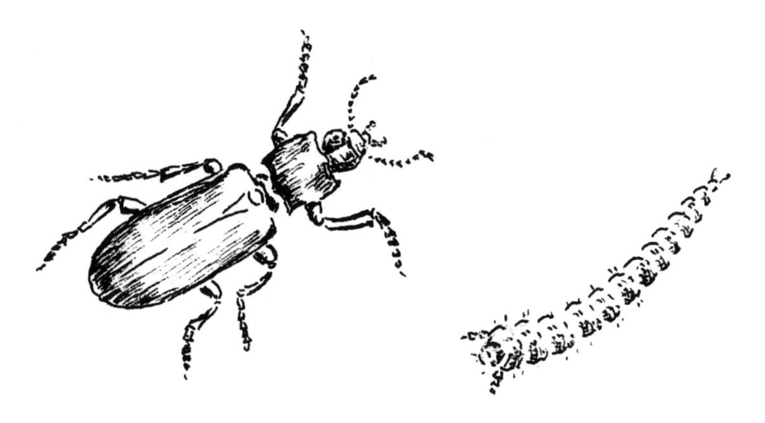

A flour beetle and larvae

Almost every barn has mice within it. There may be a few mice, there may be hundreds, but they come into a barn to eat the grains and hayseeds. No barn can be free of the grain, for the animals must eat it, nor in turn, can it be free of the mice.

Rats also come into barns. Rats, of course, are much larger than mice, and they are not, by the way, giant mice. In spite of their looks, they are not closely related to mice. Rats' high intelligence has helped them survive in spite of mankind's constant attempts to get rid of them all. For animals their size, they can quickly and easily learn complex mazes. In a barn, this means they can learn various routes and passageways that will take them safely from one end of a barn to another. Interestingly, they learn about all the objects that are near or on these pathways. If an object is moved or a new object is placed in a pathway, a rat will often avoid that pathway. (One way of keeping rats out of a house is to constantly move furniture and things around. Because of their desire for order in pathways, rats might leave the house). Once they know their pathways they can move about in the dark with great speed.

Their intelligence helps them to survive, but so does their ability to produce so many offspring. A female rat will have dozens of offspring each year. Even if all but a male and female are killed each year, the rat population can rise to high levels in months. They are also helped to survive by the fact that they are **omnivores,** which means they can eat either meat or plant food.

Fortunately for a farmer, most rats prefer to live outdoors. Barns are rarely overrun by them.

Most barns have so many mice, as well as some rats, that they attract predators. One of the most interesting of the animals that hunt mice in a barn is the barn owl. This is a whitish-colored owl with a heart-shaped face. Though many live in trees, great numbers live in barns. It is a rare barn that does not have a pair in it.

Barn owls have great survival skills. This is shown in their distribution. They are one of the very few birds that can be found almost worldwide. They live in every continent and even on offshore islands such as Curaçao and Madagascar. They survive for several reasons but mostly because of their remarkable ability to hear things. Barn owls, of all animals ever tested, can most quickly and accurately determine where a noise is coming from. They can hunt mice so well in a pitch-black barn that most people mistakenly think the owls see the mice. They do not. They hear them and know just where they are. As a mouse runs from a barn owl, the owl listens to its feet on the floor, zeroes in on the running mouse, and nabs it.

During the day, barn owls often sleep high up in a barn in a dark, out-of-the-way corner. Many barns have vents on the roof, and if owls can roost in them they will do so. They nest with their mates, which they keep as long as they live.

A barn owl

Some people are afraid of owls, but the barn owl should not be feared. It is a friend of the farmer. More than any other predator, it helps keep down mice. It does not attack humans.

Another group of predator that enters barns consists of

the rat snakes. There are several species of rat snakes, but all are similarly built. They are big and have flat abdomens and broad heads. Though non-poisonous, they often vibrate their tails but have no rattles. The most common are the corn snake, found in the Southeast and westward almost to Arizona, and the black rat snake, found in most of the eastern parts of the United States. The corn snake is yellow with rust-colored blotches on it. The black rat snake is all black, but does have mostly a white belly. Some black rat snakes may reach a length of nine feet. Rat snakes will try to bite those who touch them, so beware of them.

Adult snakes hunt rats. When a snake finds a rat it loops itself quickly over the rat and tightens its body around it, killing it by squeezing it to death. Snakes that kill in this way are called constrictors. These snakes will enter barns in search of rats, making their way in by way of cracks near the foundation. Few barns were ever tightly built, so it is easy for these snakes to find a way into a barn.

Foxes may enter barns, looking not so much for chickens as for rats and mice. There have been too many stories about foxes and their chicken-stealing habits. Yes, some foxes occasionally steal chickens; when they enter barns they do so to attack whatever they can find. The easiest animals for them to find are rats and mice. Foxes make swift work of them. In fact, few animals are so valuable to a farmer as a fox in his barn.

Other predators will come in too—long-tailed weasels, for example. These are the only weasels with brown feet and white underparts. They hunt with cunning and speed and can tackle any animal their size and win the fight. On occasion they search barns, for rodents and, rarely, a chicken.

The barn owls, mammals, and snakes search for mammals, but many birds come into a barn to hunt insects. One kind of bird preying on insects is the barn swallow. Of all the animals that live in barns, barn swallows are the loveliest. You can identify them because they are the *only* swallows in America with long, forked tails. They are remarkable fliers. They fly with amazing ease and are often seen darting in and out of the large barn doors, which are almost always kept open.

Long, long ago, before any barns were built, cliff swallows, which are closely related to barn swallows, lived in the West. As barns were built across the country, the swallows used them for nesting places. Slowly they moved eastward. Today, thanks to barns, they also live in the eastern parts of North America. They make their nests in barns, but mostly outside high on the walls, under the eaves of the roof. The small world of the barn made this major population shift of a wild animal possible. Cliff swallows can be identified because they are the only swallows that have square tails and orange rumps.

Both barn and cliff swallows eat insects found in and around the barn. On the other hand, the swallows will also fly long distances, far from the barn, to hunt insects. In its back-and-forth flights a swallow may cover hundreds of miles a day on the wing.

Pigeons are another bird almost always found in barns. They nest inside the barn up where exposed horizontal wall supports are built. They use the barn for protection and food, eating the grain that might spill to the floor.

It is probably impossible to find a barn that does not have in it common English sparrows. They too eat spilled grain.

Little brown and big brown bats often roost in barns, hanging upside down and sleeping during the day. When night falls, they fly out of the barn and hunt for night-flying insects. As they leave and enter they will, of course, nab a few barn insects.

Not only are there animals in the barn (more than can be mentioned in a book this size) but there are also plants. Mosses and algae often grow on barns; this is why barn roofs often look green. Mushrooms may grow in dung. Lichens may grow on the rocks that form the foundation of a barn.

In the dank areas of a barn one can often find worms, sow bugs, and in dark corners many, many spiders.

A barn is a living world filled with tremendous activity, more than meets the eye. It is a place where men, women, and their animals come in contact with the world of the wild.

·7·

A Waterfall Spray Area

As water falls, foam bubbles up and fine spray drifts off in the wind. The foglike spray will constantly dampen trees, rocks, cliffs, ferns all around a waterfall. Near big waterfalls spray falls like a rain that lasts tens of thousands of years.

Because of the constant moisture and the springs from underground water, areas near waterfalls have special plants, many rarely if ever found anyplace else. It is a world all to itself. This is especially true if waterfalls pour into hidden glens, which are small steep-sided canyons often lost to the rest of the world and rarely visited.

Spray areas are ideal places for certain primitive plants, such as algae, mosses, and liverworts, that reproduce by means of sperm rather than pollen. Like animal sperm, the plant sperm must swim by means of a wiggling tail in a fluid substance before they can reach and fertilize a plant egg. In many cases the egg can also swim about, exactly like the sperm. Since swimming sperm and eggs need a watery fluid, the plants need to be in places where there is a great deal of moisture.

Botanists sometimes say that mosses, liverworts, and

some algae, because of their need for water and moisture, are the amphibians of the plant world.

The most primitive plants that one can see without the aid of a microscope are the algae. Since they contain chlorophyll, freshwater algae, with few exceptions, are green—many a beautiful color, greenest of the greens. Lacking any hint of true roots, stems, and leaves, they have very simple shapes. One type, filament algae, lives in the water itself or on constantly wet rocks or logs. Since a filament is a thread, the alga can be identified by its shape of long threads, often tangled together. Beware of it, for it is amazingly slippery stuff. The most common genera, *Ulothrix* and *Oedogonium,* grow on wet stones and sticks and even on living plants. Another, *Draparnaldia,* grows near cold springs that often seep from rocks near waterfalls. Algae appeared on earth almost a billion years ago. To touch an alga is like touching a prehistoric plant.

A slightly more highly evolved plant is the lichen. This dual plant is actually part alga and part fungus. Many lichens can grow in extremely dry areas; others do best in constantly moist areas. Rocks may be partly covered with a lichen called rock tripe. It is a dark olive-brown color and looks somewhat like a leaf of dark lettuce. (This lichen is edible, and people lost in the wilderness have sometimes survived by eating it.)

One can often find mosses growing in perpetually moist areas. They have leaflike green scales (moss "leaves" are called thalli), which unlike the true leaves of higher plants lack veins and other important structures. On most mosses there are **sporophytes,** composed of tiny stalks called **setae** tipped with an urn-shaped **spore** container called a **capsule.** Sometimes sporophytes lack stalks and can be located nesting in the thalli. Water mosses, which grow submerged in water, is one of these. A hand lens helps one study mosses. Look especially for one called "delicate fern moss." It lies flat and has fragile-looking leaves.

Star mosses form lovely leaf patterns. The leaves point outward from the stem of the moss, forming the star patterns that give the moss its common name. These plants rarely grow more than an inch in height. Rising from the plants are wiry little setae topped with football-shaped capsules. In the course of millions of years star mosses have spread to three continents in the northern regions of the temperate zone. This widespread geographic range is the sign of a truly successful plant.

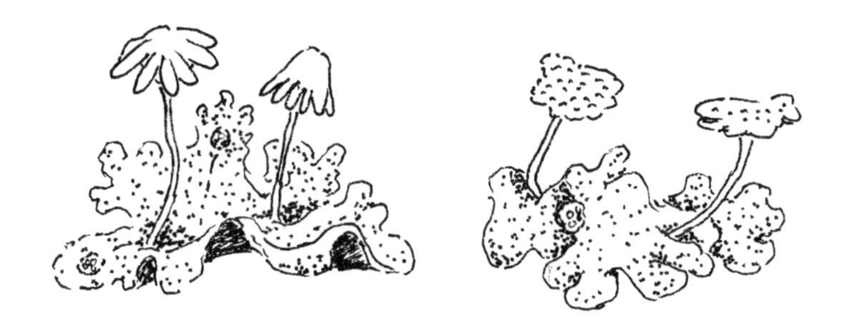

The common liverwort

All mosses, even those in dry regions, need water around them so that the sperm can swim to female eggs. Desert mosses depend on heavy seasonal rains. Waterfall mosses have it easier.

Liverworts and hornworts are closely related to mosses, but one can see differences. Liverworts and hornworts usually have flat "leaves" or thalli, which resemble chunks of lettuce dropped on the ground. The sporophyte capsules, like those of most mosses, are on stalks but are *not* urn-shaped. Often they are umbrella-shaped. The common hornwort has the unusual distinction of being found all over the world. Its sporophyte resembles a three-pronged fork. The thallus has what appear to be roots but are actually rhizoids, whose function is merely to hold the plant in place on moist soil. Unlike a real root it does not transport water from the soil into the thallus. (Differences between liverworts and hornworts are too slight to be of concern to us.)

The stems of horsetails are straight and segmented, much the way bamboo stems are. The three-sided leaves look like bristles. The fruit is a hard cone. Before the time of the dinosaurs, huge forests of horsetail "trees," reaching a hundred feet high, helped produce coal as they fell into swamps and were later covered with mud and then solid rock. Field horsetail is between eight and twenty inches high. In the spring pink stems appear with cones on them.

Millions of years ago huge forests of fern trees grew in and around swamps. Today most ferns live in drier locales, but some remain in very moist places, such as waterfall spray areas. One seen often is the common polypody fern. The bumplike **sori,** which hold the spore (reproduction organs) of the fern, look like tiny red-brown buttons on the underside of the leaflets. This fern rarely grows to be a foot in height. Thick stands of it make for beautiful lacy areas near water.

Many people consider the maidenhair fern to be the most beautiful of all. Its stem is black and shiny and may loop until it is almost horseshoe shaped. The ferns grow to be about twenty inches tall.

In addition to the primitive amphibian plants, some flowering plants also live in waterfall spray areas, though they must adapt to such a wet world. One change is in their leaves. Leaves take in and let out gases, such as oxygen, carbon dioxide, and gaseous water vapor, through holes called stomata. Leaves of plants in moist areas have more stomata so that they can get rid of water vapors more easily. These leaves also have more lobes to help them drain off water. (Plainsmen and mountain men wore buckskin jackets decorated with fringes. Those fringes were not just decoration; they helped drain water off the jackets.)

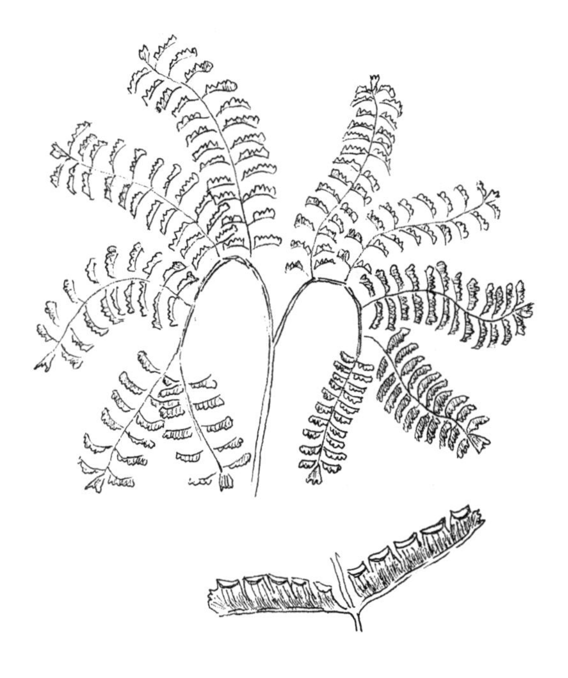

Maidenhair fern

Because waterfall areas are often shady areas, as though in twilight, the flowering plants in those places have larger-than-normal-sized leaves to catch as much light as possible.

Many plants that live in bright sunlight, such as desert plants, have very small leaves. (Cactus, in fact, lost their leaves millions of years ago.) Those desert plants that have leaves often turn their leaves 180 degrees so that sunlight touches only the edges and often have thick leaf coverings as protection from drying winds and dust. Plants in moist, shady places, however, turn their leaves 90 degrees in order to catch the maximum amount of light. Usually they have thin leaves. Some, too, have special structures that carry air and vital oxygen to their roots so that the roots can be ventilated and not become waterlogged.

A plant that lives in constantly moist places and has made adaptations in its structure so that it can survive in such a place is called a **hydrophyte.** (*Hydro* means water and *phyte* means plants, so the term means waterplant.) The internal chemistry of the plants varies, too, but a description of those processes is beyond the scope of this book.

Trillium are plants of the lily family. They have large leaves, always three and only three, and the flower has three petals. They bloom in spring, one of the most dramatic of wild flowers.

Skunk cabbages, too, grow in moist soil. This plant, which appears in early spring, has a large single leaf that forms a hood over the flowering stalk of the plant. It can be identified by its foul smell.

Buttercups have bright-yellow petals, so smooth and shiny that they look as if they could be made of plastic. The shape of the leaves resembles a bird's foot. Buttercups grow in very damp areas and can thrive even if partly submerged in water for periods of time.

Red osier dogwood shrubs often grow in moist places.

Look for them in early spring, when their bark turns a bright red.

Willows can baffle even expert botanists; it is extremely difficult to identify the species. Willow shrubs and trees have long, thin leaves. The "pussies" of pussy willows are actually flower clusters called catkins, but one would not recognize them as flowers since they have no petals.

Rhododendrons are shrubs and trees that have lovely pink or red five-petaled flowers in big clusters. The fruit is thin and sticky. Rhododendron leaves are dark green and shiny and have smooth edges. These trees often grow in glens.

A rhododendron blossom

The witch hazel shrub is the source of the commonly used lotion named for it. The shrub has that peculiar witch hazel smell. These shrubs often grown in crooked masses, their branches going this way and that in random, crazy ways. The slightly-notched leaves, almost as wide as they are long, turn yellow in the fall. The witch hazel shrub blooms late in the year, often in October. The yellow flowers have distinct, long, ribbonlike petals. No other flowers bloom so late.

A person walking in a glen, perhaps near a waterfall, might well be surprised to see that tall trees grow in such restricted places. Some, such as tulip trees, maples, oaks, and evergreens, may reach heights of over one hundred feet. Though at first puzzling, it is easy to explain. The need for more light forces the trees to grow taller so that their tops can reach above the walls of the glen and the upper leaves can enjoy full sunlight.

We have seen that near waterfall spray areas one can find ancient plants. Ancient animal types are present there as well. In a way, such an area is part of a prehistoric world. To walk in it is to walk back in time.

Before we take a look at individual animal species, it must be mentioned that there is not a great deal in such places that would attract animals. It is mainly a green world of unusual plants. Some flowering shrubs and a few wild flowers produce nectar. A few bushes and trees have nuts and berries. Insect life is not rich. Most insects that live near water prefer still water, rather than rushing streams and waterfalls.

About three hundred million years ago great changes were beginning to occur in the world. Fish were living in the oceans and lakes, but no four-legged animals were living on land. Great forests of giant horsetails and other plants were potential food supplies for land animals if they came ashore. But which of them could come ashore? Actually some fish did waddle ashore, probably walking on strong fins. They breathed air through their air sacs. Slowly over millions of years fish became amphibians. Fins turned into legs and air sacs into lungs. These amphibians must be near water. First, they lay their eggs in water and no place else. Second, most spend part of their lives as water-dwelling creatures. Many young amphibians have gills, which they later lose when they develop lungs. Unlike reptiles, their close relatives, they have slimy skin which, for most species, needs to be constantly moist.

Salamanders, which are tailed amphibians, have a long, long history. About 100,000,000 years ago, through the process of **evolution,** true salamanders appeared. They may wander from watery places and live near and under damp leaves, but they must always return to the water. Some species can be found near waterfalls. Several prefer rapidly running streams. They also inhabit out-of-the-way glens.

Salamanders resemble ancient four-legged creatures. When you see a salamander you are looking back hundreds of millions of years to a primitive creature. Among the most common species one might find near waterfall areas are the spring (sometimes called purple) and red salamanders. The young red salamanders are unmistakable, very red with black spots. As adults they turn browner. They are about six and a half inches long. They often live in cold springs, such as those found near waterfalls. Though spring salamanders might be purplish in color, they can also be yellowish-brown. They are slightly bigger than the red salamanders, being about eight and a half inches in length. They are found in hilly country, near cold springs and streams. Salamanders eat insects and insect eggs.

Dusky salamanders often stay among mosses and rocks near streams. Because they are only about six inches long and gray, greenish, or brown in color, they are hard to find. This species has a gold rim around the pupil of the eye. They are good climbers and might be found working their way up steep cliffs.

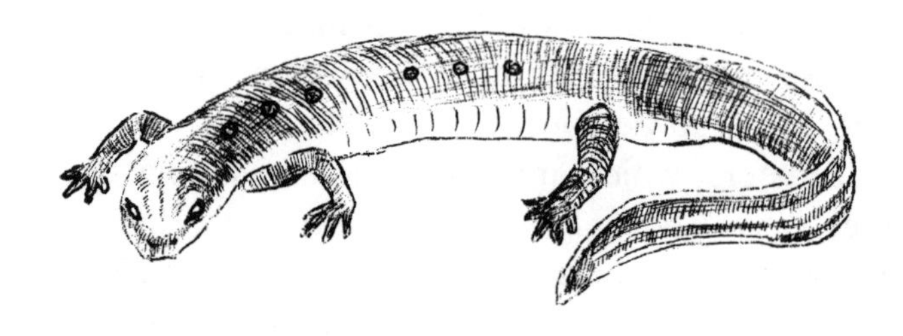

A salamander

Salamanders called newts spend their early months in water and have external gills. They lose their gills and then move on land to live for two to three years, during which time they are known as efts. Later on, they move back into the water as full adults and spend the rest of their lives in the water again. The land-dwelling eft is orange-red with black dots. The water-dwelling newt is the only aquatic salamander to be green in color with red spots.

Frogs, unlike the above-mentioned salamanders, prefer quiet water, such as that found in ponds and pools. Nevertheless, a few that travel about on land or climb trees may stray into spray areas. Those frogs you see near waterfall spray areas are wanderers rather than inhabitants.

Many waterfall areas lie in hidden glens. There is a lost-world aspect to such places. Everything seems private, hidden, secret, and timeless. Glens offer many birds the privacy they need. Among these shy little birds, which mostly stay hidden in glens, are the veeries. They are found only in places densely covered with shrubs. Veeries are small thrushes that resemble robins without red breasts. One rarely sees the veery, but one can sometimes hear its song, which sounds like *vee yur, vee yur, veer, veer.*

The Louisiana waterthrush, in spite of its name, is not a thrush but a warbler. These chickadee-sized birds live near waterfalls and flowing streams. They have a distinct white eye line and unstreaked throats. Like a sandpiper, it teeters as it walks, often running along the sides of streams. Its song is a complex jumble of notes but strong and wild.

The tufted titmouse is a lovely little bird, the only gray bird that has a distinct crest. Everything about it shows delicacy. Its song is distinct, sounding like *Peter Peter Peter* very rapidly. Though a bird of wild glens, it is also often seen in backyards and city parks.

The golden-winged warbler, like all warblers, rarely stays still for more than a few seconds. It is the only warbler that has a dark bib and also a golden wing patch. This little bird is sometimes seen hanging by its feet upside down on the tips of branches. Its song is *see buzz-buzz-buzz.*

Quite often cliff swallows are seen flying near waterfalls. They nest on steep cliffs, but not necessarily near waterfalls. They fly by the waterfalls as they hunt for insects. They are the only swallows with buff-colored rumps and square tails.

In general, mammals avoid waterfall areas. They are too wet and cold, and the rocks are too steep and slippery. River otters, however, may roam through such places.

They live like gypsies, always on the move. Although they are large, they are hard to see because they prefer to stay in hidden areas.

Few animals play. Humans can be playful; so can dolphins, chimpanzees, and, oddly enough, some birds. Otherwise, playfulness is a rare trait in nature. Otters, however, not only play but make slides for themselves. These slides, usually open, steep, muddy slopes, entertain otters for hours on end. Up they go and, *whoosh,* down they go, just like children in a playground. Perhaps because of their playful nature, they sometimes befriend humans.

Otters do not spend all their time being playful. Quite the opposite. They keep a wary eye open, stay hidden, and can hunt better than almost any other animal. Otters avoid fights, but if in a fight an otter can and will kill any animal its size. Mostly, they hunt frogs and crayfish.

Minks are weasels, as are otters. They are small, slender mammals, all brown except for a white spot under the chin. They have bright eyes and are expert hunters, seeking small mammals, birds, fish, and frogs. They climb well and can move easily in and out of steep-sided glens. Though they are more common than one would expect, they are difficult to see, for they stay well hidden and often hunt at night.

A waterfall spray area represents for the most part a shadowy world, always lost in a half-twilight. It is a peculiar and fascinating small world, quite unlike any other, an unusual one to explore.

·8·

A Tree

For many animals and a few plants a single, isolated tree serves as their environment, their home, their feeding place. If you wish to explore a truly remarkable small world, you need to walk no farther than to the nearest tree.

A tree is a living being with a life history. At one time it was a seed, then a sprout, and given enough time, a tree—perhaps even a very large one. After tens, hundreds—or occasionally, for such trees as sequoias and bristlecone pines, thousands—of years, the tree dies and falls to the ground. Then, for a while, usually for many years, it is a log. In time the log disappears.

Aside from some highly unusual trees such as the ginkgo, all trees start as seeds. The conifers, such as pines and junipers, produce seeds from cones; other trees, such as maples and pear trees, produce seeds from flowers. A few—an amazingly few—seeds that fall on the ground will ever sprout. Few that sprout will ever become trees. Some small trees grow from runners, long underground stems that look like roots.

Young trees are often damaged or eaten by animals. When you see a large tree that lacks branches on the lower part of the trunk, it is usually because deer, cows, and horses have eaten away whatever branches they could reach. Trees in pastures typically lack lower branches.

Fortunately, the vast majority of trees survive attacks when young and grow to the point where they can produce flowers or cones. When they do the story changes.

The flowers of many trees contain rich nectar, which lures many insects to them. Basswood or linden trees in particular have wonderful nectar. Their flowers grow out of the center of the leaf. Honeybees, lured to the flowers by sight as well as by fragrance, change the nectar into a delicious honey. Other trees that produce good honey are catalpa and tupelo (or black gum). Identify catalpas by their very large heart-shaped leaves and long beans. Tupelo trees have shiny leaves with smooth edges. Their green flowers are small, and so is their oval blue fruit. The bark often has small rectangular blocks on it.

Sometimes wild honeybees make colonies inside old trees and store their honey in honeycombs. During the day butterflies will also sip nectar, and at night so will moths.

After the flowers have bloomed, nuts, berries, and fruits develop. They lure many more insects, birds, and mammals to the trees. Starlings (these are the only birds that are dark in color and have short tails), crows, all kinds of jays, orchard orioles (these have deep chestnut-colored breasts, bellies, and rumps), cardinals, and many others eat the fruit and berries of trees. Raccoons, deer, and other mammals also eat nuts, fruits, and berries. Squirrels eat nuts and acorns.

Cedar waxwings (the only crested brown birds lacking white on their wings) eat juniper and cedar berries. So do grouse, which are chicken-sized brown birds with fan-shaped tails. Crossbills (the only birds with crossed bills) eat pinecone seeds.

Fruits, nuts, and berries also feed numerous insect larvae. The worm you find in your apple is not at related to an earthworm. It is a caterpillar, probably that of a codling moth. Codling moths are brown moths that have a yellow chevron at the tip of each forewing. The holes in acorns and all other edible nuts are those of nut weevils, which have yellow-green bodies, long legs, and unbelievably long "snouts."

Trees provide many insects with yet another source of food, namely leaves. The primary eaters of leaves are caterpillars of butterflies and moths. The leaves of elm, poplar, hackberry, and willows are eaten by caterpillars of the black mourning cloak butterfly. It has black wings decorated with red dots and bristles. The green caterpillars of anglewing butterflies—their wings, which look deeply torn on the edges, are reddish-orange with black dots—feed on elm leaves. Tiger swallowtails are large, mostly yellow butterflies with wingspans of almost four inches. Their green caterpillars, which have one yellow band and fake eye marks, eat wild cherry leaves. Other caterpillars eat the leaves of birch, oak, hickory, maple, catalpa, and willow trees.

Walking sticks must be seen to be believed. Though they look just like sticks, they are insects that walk about on stems of oak, locust, cherry, and walnut trees looking for leaves to eat. These insects resemble sticks so well that, though they are common, few people ever see them.

Spittlebugs are also startling. The foam they make on stems of plants resembles spittle. Actually the foam protects the insects' **nymphs** (wingless immature young) as they feed.

The katydid, a type of grasshopper that calls out *Katydid-she did-katy did* in the summertime, eats leaves, usually feeding on those of cherry, oak, apple, and maple trees.

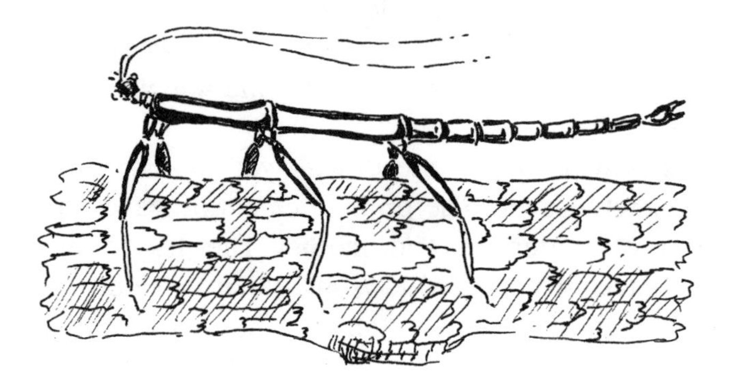

A walking stick

The easiest-seen leaf eaters are the tent caterpillars and fall webworms. Tent caterpillars build their tents in the spring in the place where branches and stems meet. Webworms build theirs in the fall over clusters of leaves.

Insects not only eat leaves but suck sap from trees. A strange and surprising one is the scale insect. One might think that little scales on tree twigs are deformities in the bark of the twig. Actually this is the covering for the scale insect hidden and protected below. It sucks sap from fruit trees, sometimes damaging them.

If you use your imagination you can see how buffalo tree hoppers got their name. These small green sap-sucking insects have humps that resemble those of American buffaloes. Note that they can hop, too.

Below the ground, tree roots can be attacked by various hungry beetle larvae, called grubs. Black *Prionus* beetles, which are about one and a half inches long, carry magnificent, thick, scaly antennae. Their grubs eat tree roots and often damage orchard and ornamental trees. Flatheaded and long-horned borers come in many varieties and rate as some of the most beautiful and colorful of American beetles. The long-horned borers bore into the wood of trees and can be serious pests of orchard and conifer forest trees. The larvae of flatheaded beetles feed between bark and wood.

Moles, small mammals that dig long underground tunnels, also damage tree roots. One would think that all these creatures would eat every last tree away. Sometimes the insects do win and leave large forests of dead trees behind, but trees can, in their own way, fight back. They do so in several ways. First, most tree leaves taste bitter and some contain poisons. Peach tree leaves can kill humans as well as insects. Some seeds are poisonous; apple and some apricot seeds contain one of the most powerful poisons of all—cyanide. Though maple sugar sap is sweet, most tree sap is bitter. Pine trees have resin and gums that ward off insect attacks. Thick bark acts as a barrier to most insect and bird attacks. To some extent trees can heal themselves.

More than anything, the balance of nature itself protects trees. Insects that survive by eating tree leaves, nuts, berries, and roots do so in order to live. If these insects succeeded in killing all the trees, what would they eat? In order to survive, insects must keep the trees alive. Over millions of years a balance has been worked out. The insects eat only what they need and stop short of killing off all trees.

Occasionally mistakes happen. When a species of insect gets the upper hand and kills off a forest of trees, the insects thrive and get plenty to eat—but their young die. Millions upon millions of insects of the next generation in that forest starve to death. (Fortunately birds and mammals can leave the devastated forest to live someplace else.)

This cycle of feast and famine takes place all through nature. The classic example is the relationship between snowshoe rabbits and lynx in the North. When there are great numbers of rabbits, lynx do well and more young than normal survive into adulthood. The larger number of adult lynxes hunt the numerous rabbits and soon eat too many. The rabbit population drops. The next generation of lynxes starves and the young rarely become adults. Free of being hunted by lynxes, the rabbit population swells, and the cycle continues.

Trees benefit from other struggles. Insects that eat trees are in turn eaten by other insects or birds or mammals. A goodly number of them also die of fungus and bacteria and viral attacks. So, trees survive because of this balance between the hunter and the hunted.

Trees provide animals with benefits other than food—perches, for instance. Many types of birds perch in trees. Some sleep while perched on waving branches. They can do this balancing act because while they sleep, some muscles, instead of relaxing, tighten and hold the birds.

Ask almost anyone what he thinks of in connection with a tree, and he'll probably answer, "Birds." Interestingly, this relationship between birds and trees goes back to prehistoric times. The earliest birds, such as *Archaeopteryx* of about 150 million years ago, developed from a line of dinosaurs. (Strictly speaking, today's birds are a type of dinosaur and some zoologists think that they should be called "dinosauria.") The earliest birds were not fliers; at best they only glided. To learn how to glide, they needed to climb trees and leap off into the air. Once gliding was mastered over millions of years, they learned how to fly. Today, of course, birds and trees have a natural relationship, but let us not carry that relationship too far. Numerous bird species of today—gulls, ducks, horned larks, many types of sparrows—never get near a tree. And after learning the art of flight, many species of birds ignored trees thereafter.

A Baltimore oriole and its nest

Even so, trees provide nesting places for many birds. Some easily found tree-nesting birds should be mentioned. Male Baltimore orioles are the only birds in America that are orange and have a black head and black throat. The females are drab, mostly a brownish olive, with white wing bars and dull orange rumps. They make beautiful, hanging nests of carefully woven grasses and can be found on orchard trees and others. On first seeing such a remarkable nest a person might think that it was made by a human basket weaver. Baltimore orioles lay white eggs with scribbly black-and-brown markings.

Robins make cup-shaped nests of grass and mud in the sturdy crotches of trees where branches start. They lay blue eggs. Blue jays make cruder-looking nests of twigs put together helter-skelter on branches near trunks. Their eggs are olive-colored, often with brown markings.

Many other birds also use trees for nesting, for laying eggs, and raising their young. Actually this use of a tree is a life-and-death matter for the survival of bird species. No trees, no nest, no future generations. These birds are totally dependent on the trees.

Birds are also attracted to trees because of the vast numbers of insects near or on them. The insects on a tree determine where birds will spend time. For example, many insects live in the leafy clutter found beneath trees. Birds that hunt them, such as the ovenbirds (identified by their call, *Teacher, TEACHER*), and rufous-sided towhees (the only birds with black hoods and backs and red-brown sides) spend almost all their time scratching about in the leaves and rarely fly into the branches of the tree.

Birds that pick out insect eggs from the bark of trees or that hunt insects such as ants and beetles walking up and down tree trunks will hunt them on the trunks and rarely be seen anyplace else. Typical of these birds are the nuthatches, woodpeckers, and sapsuckers, a type of woodpecker.

Flycatchers, which are small, quick-flying birds with thin, small beaks, must see their prey (not just flies, but also wasps, mosquitoes, and bees) flying by trees. They need to have a place to observe things around them, so they stay on the tops of trees or on the outer tips of tree branches. So do hawks, especially sparrow hawks. (See Chapter Eleven for a description of sparrow hawks.)

A few mammals need trees as places to live and to build nests. They need protection from predators, such as foxes, bears, and snakes.

A flying squirrel

One animal that lives in trees is highly unusual. It is the flying squirrel of eastern North America. Actually there are two species, the northern flying squirrel and the southern flying squirrel. They do not actually fly but glide from tree to tree on folds of skin that stretch from front legs to back legs. The best time to see them gliding is during the light of the full moon, for they become more active then. Flying squirrels live in holes in trees, often very high from the ground. If you knock on a tree that has such a squirrel hole, the little squirrel might peek out its hole at you.

Everyone is familiar with the common gray squirrels that

spend their lives in trees and make nests in them. (See Chapter Nine for more about gray squirrels.) Raccoons and skunks and opossums often use holes in trees for shelter.

Hornets often build large paper nests in trees, so they too share in the small world of a tree. Beware of these nests. *Do not play with one.*

Quite a number of insects build cocoons that they place on trees. One of the most curious of cocoons belongs to a moth that does not look like a moth, namely a bagworm. The wings of these moths are semitransparent. All over their cocoons are tiny sticks glued together, giving them a log-cabin look, except that the "logs" stand upright. Other cocoons can commonly be found on trees, and so can egg masses of many insects and spiders.

Eastern fence lizards often climb about in trees. So do many different small frogs, such as the spring peepers whose calls can so often be heard in the springtime. This frog, which is gray and has an X on its back, is extremely difficult to find because it is so small that it can sit on an average postage stamp and because it is difficult to see when it is high in a tree.

As a tree gets old, its defenses, mainly its sap and bark covering, weaken. More and more beetles attack it, many boring into the wood. Termites make chambers in the wood. Fungus, too, attacks a tree. Shelf fungus will grow outward, horizontally from the exposed wood, to form shelves. Mushrooms will spring up on the exposed tops of the dead roots.

Eventually trees die. Most die by stages. This limb and then that limb gets rotten and falls off. During its last years a tree may stand almost without limbs. Then some windy night it will fall over.

When the tree collapses it will lie on the ground as a log. Horn and staghorn beetle larvae will enter into its wood. Rats, mice, raccoons, and other animals may live in a hollow in the log. Spiders will weave webs over the entrances to holes. Dry rot, which can be caused by any number of fungi, usually **Polypore**, will turn the log into a powdery dust. Polypores are hard shelf fungi. This dust will provide the soil with nutriments: proteins and minerals that the old tree once held in its leaves, trunk, and branches.

Some day a new tree will grow where the old tree stood. It will use those valuable proteins and minerals to grow healthy and strong. Thus each tree will be in turn followed by another.

·9·

A Vacant Lot

Vacant lots come and go. For decades a building may stand in the midst of a city. Then, one day, a wrecking crew starts taking it down and soon leaves a vacant lot. In another part of the city, a lot that has never had a building on it is cleared. Within weeks a building goes up and will cover that lot for decades, perhaps for a century or longer.

Not only do vacant lots come and go, they may exist for only a matter of days if one building comes down and another is quickly built on top of it. On the other hand, a vacant lot may remain for years, or decades or longer before a building is placed on it.

Whatever the case may be, almost all vacant lots have a history. It is, for most, like a story that has a beginning and an end.

Let's explore the history of a typical vacant lot. After a building comes down bulldozers "clean up" the lot, fill in the basement, and smooth away piles of dirt. The rubble is hauled off. What is left is a plot of land, smoothed, bare, with not a single plant growing on it.

On rare occasions seeds may remain under buildings for decades, perhaps a hundred years or more. The building over them keeps them dry and preserved. Once the building goes, rainwater may dampen the seeds and cause them to sprout. When this happens, new plants will start growing in the vacant lot.

This sort of thing happened in London during World War II. After German warplanes bombed parts of London and buildings were damaged and torn down, plants that had not been known to grow in London for hundreds of years started growing in the vacant lots. Many beautiful wild flowers sprang up from old, hidden, preserved seeds.

Some seeds of the arctic tundra lupine, 10,000 years old, were found in frozen ground. Once replanted and warmed up, they germinated in forty-eight hours.

Even if this does not happen with old seeds, plants will show up anyway. Some of the seeds will be carried in the wind to the newly formed vacant lot. Birds, such as common pigeons, blue jays, and English sparrows will leave undigested seeds on the ground in their droppings. Seeds may drop off trucks from the countryside. Other seeds may drop off the clothing of people walking near or across the vacant lot. Eventually seeds of plants and spores of mosses and ferns will find their way to the lot.

The first plants that grow will be **annuals:** typically ragweeds, clovers, dandelions, hawkweeds, red clover, Queen Anne's lace, smartweeds, many species of mustards, horehound, and other weeds. There may be some mosses.

Dandelions are known to all. So is red clover, which has the typical clover leaf. The others need explanations.

Ragweeds are large, tall weeds, some growing ten feet tall, with numerous branches and fernlike leaves and tiny green flowers.

Black-eyed Susans are tall daisylike yellow flowers with

chocolate-colored central disks. They may grow to three feet high.

Hawkweeds have dandelion-shaped flowers and leaves, but the flower grows on top of a long stem. Hawkweeds vary, but many have orange-colored flowers.

Queen Anne's lace is a wild carrot that can grow to be three feet high. It has a cluster of white flowers held high above the rest of the plant. Often the middle flower is red, purple, or black. This single flower identifies it.

A black-eyed Susan

Smartweeds rarely grow to be a foot high and are usually half that height. Pink flowers grow in a thick plumelike cluster. The leaves of the plant are long and thin, like willow leaves. It is called a smartweed because of its sting. Some people are allergic to this plant.

There are many types of mustard plants, usually having

yellow or white flowers. All the flowers have four petals arranged in the shape of a cross.

In a summer or two a vacant lot will be partly covered with weeds, wild flowers, and grasses, such as timothy grass and crabgrass.

Timothy grass shows itself best in June, when the flowering spikes thicken. (The flowers of this, and all grasses, are different from most flowers for they lack petals and have different structures.) The flowering spike is dense and thick. Look at it. In strong sunlight parts of it twinkle, bejewelled.

Crabgrass is topped with five or six spikes that look like tines on a fork. Many people confuse it with Bermuda grass, which at first glance it resembles. You can tell them apart, however, because crabgrass has rough leaves covered with hairs. Bermuda grass has smooth, stiff, light-green leaves. Crabgrass is an annual, but Bermuda grass is a **perennial**.

Many vacant lots remain in constant shade because tall buildings always block out the sunlight. Ferns may grow in these shady areas. One fern commonly found in the shade is the Christmas fern. It appears early in spring when its "fiddleheads" rise above the ground. It has long fronds that may grow to thirty inches in length. On the underside of larger leaves are two rows of small buttonlike objects. These sori contain the reproductive spores of the fern. It is called Christmas fern because it is evergreen and often used in Christmas wreaths.

On damp surfaces, certain types of algae will grow. One of the most commonly seen is *Protococcus,* which in early spring often covers stones and wooden boards with a bright Kelly-green color. It is often the first sign of spring.

Quite a number of plants can establish themselves in a vacant lot, but they must be tough to withstand a harsh environment. All the plants that grow in a vacant lot must, to some degree, put up with pollution. Certainly gasoline fumes, industrial fumes, street dust, and other products of our civilization will be in the air. Tall buildings will block the light for many plants and can also force the wind to blow between them like a gale over a vacant lot. The soil may lack many minerals the plants need. Worse, it may contain oils, chemicals, and other waste products. The plants must contend with trash and often with smoke from incinerators.

Moreover, people often make paths that cross or criss-cross vacant lots. These paths are usually barren and hard, and few if any plants will grow there, partly because plants are physically damaged but even more so because the soil is impacted. Roots have trouble moving in hard soil, and oxygen cannot reach the roots when the soil is packed tightly.

When the first year's plants bloom, their flowers produce nectar and later seeds, both of which attract insects and birds. Of all the insects that will come into the vacant lot butterflies will be the most easily seen, and one of the most common is the cabbage butterfly. It has a wingspan of about an inch and a half, and it is pure white, except for some black markings on the tips of the forewings. Cabbage butterflies can be seen all over the continental United States and even in southern Alaska. Their larvae eat common mustard plants.

A butterfly often seen in the early spring, and sometimes even in the middle of the winter, is the mourning cloak. This is a dark-purple butterfly, its wings edged with yellow and also dotted with blue near the band. Its larvae eat elm, poplar, and willow leaves. Large, with a wingspan of over three inches, the mourning cloaks add beauty to vacant lots.

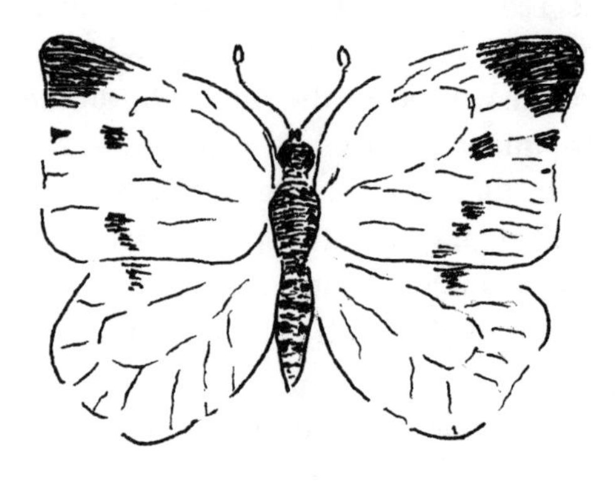

A cabbage butterfly

At times grasshoppers invade vacant lots to eat on grasses and other plants. They and their close relatives, the crickets and locusts, can fill a summer afternoon with dozens of different types of songs. Sometimes vacant lots in the heart of New York City, Chicago, or Los Angeles buzz with their songs. Actually these are not songs at all but mating calls. Males rub their legs together and females, hearing the buzz, become attracted to the males and go find them. Each species of grasshopper or cricket has its own song. (Katydid: *Katy did-she did-Katy did.* Meadow grasshoppers: *Tsip-tsip-tsip-tsip.* Black field crickets: *Treat-treat-treat-treat.* Small ground crickets: *Ti-ti-ti-ti.*)

Ants appear quickly in almost all vacant lots. One species is the little black ant. The workers, the ones most commonly seen, are only about one-sixteenth of an inch in length. They often use their little paths over and over again. You can see long lines of them moving single file, one after the other along one of their paths. In spring or fall, one might see the winged queens and winged males in flight. During their flight they mate and the queens later establish a new colony.

Bumblebees will fly from flower to flower. They make colonies in holes, which may be old, unused mouseholes, but could be almost any convenient hole.

Because most vacant lots are littered one almost always finds flies, usually the common housefly. The female lays its eggs in rotting garbage.

A praying mantis

One insect in a vacant lot will be a small beetle known to everyone, the ladybug. It hunts other insects, mostly the harmful ones. Much less known is the praying mantis. This strange-looking creature is long, thin, and green. Its long back legs bend like grasshopper legs. It has a triangular-shaped head. Oddly, it can move its head. Some say it is the only insect that can look over its shoulder.

The praying mantis waits patiently for insects to fly near it. Because of its color and "sticklike" appearance, insects probably do not see it. Once an insect comes near, the powerful praying mantis grabs it with its barbed front legs.

Other creatures that hunt insects in vacant lots are spiders. Garden spiders make beautiful, and at times, dramatic webs. There are 120 species of American garden spiders. All have long legs, and most of them are covered with colorful spots, many being black and yellow-orange.

A garden spider

To make a web, the spider attaches its silk to a branch, then tries to let the wind carry the other end to hook on to another branch. If it cannot do so, it walks down the first branch, climbs the other one, and pulls the silk tightly. Then it walks across the thread, which acts as a bridge. The spider descends from the middle of the bridge thread and drops to the ground suspended on another thread. It pulls on the vertical thread until it and the bridge threads form a three-threaded Y. Then the spider connects other threads, radiating from the center of the Y. Once radiating threads are in place, it will weave spiralling threads onto them. Then the web is done, and the spider waits until an insect flies or jumps into it.

Earthworms will multiply in a vacant lot. Often you can find them with a flashlight when they emerge from their holes at night, especially after it has rained.

One animal that will probably be found is De Kay's snake, also called the brown snake. It has a plain pale belly and two lines of small dots down its brown back. It is a small snake that hunts spiders and insects. Many city children know this snake, which is hardly much bigger than an earthworm.

In the fall seed-eating birds will come into the vacant lot. One such bird will almost invariably be the English sparrow, the most common bird of any city. It is a small sparrow (actually a finch) with a black bib. It eats seeds, insects, garbage—in fact, almost anything.

Common pigeons are very well suited for city living. The tall buildings offer them nesting ledges. They know how to take off rapidly and how to fly swiftly about in a small space, such as a vacant lot. Actually, few birds in the world can fly faster than these pigeons.

During the next few years after a vacant lot has come into existence, and the annuals have become common, perennials and woody plants will show up. Often poison ivy will start growing. This plant, which can be a bush or a vine, has three leaves that grow together. They are most often shiny. The plant is poisonous and can cause severe skin rashes. Though poisonous to us, the seeds are safe for birds to eat.

Another vine is the Virginia creeper. Its notched leaves come in clusters of five. The flowers are hardly noticeable, but in the fall blue berries appear on the vines. Birds and mammals will eat them.

In sunny open vacant lots white pines may appear, as they so often do in abandoned fields. These pines have bundles of five needles and long cones.

The white pine: needles, cone, and tree

Gray birch and sumac trees may spring up, but the most common tree of vacant lots is the ailanthus, also called the tree of heaven. It was discovered around 1750 by Pierre Nicholas Le Cheron d'Incarville someplace north of Peking, China. He did not call it a tree of heaven, but rather, a stinking ash. The tree has fernlike leaves. Crushed between the fingers, the leaves seem to most people to have an unpleasant odor. Unlike most other trees or plants, the ailanthus has separate male and female trees, each having a different type of flower. The female produces a distinct twisted light-brown fruit, which hangs in clusters. Male trees lack the twisted fruit and instead have small yellow-green roundish flowers.

As time goes on and the trees grow, many vacant lots become littered with tin cans and other types of trash. The damp places under boards may soon be inhabited by spiders, perhaps centipedes, beetles, and sow bugs (also called pill bugs).

The ancestors of sow bugs lived in the oceans several hundred million years ago. In fact, several ocean creatures today are closely related to sow bugs and look like them. There is also a freshwater sow bug. Because these creatures never really adapted well to living on the land and in fact are not yet true land animals, they must always stay in damp places. This is why one can find them under damp rubbish and litter.

Once a vacant lot has trees and shrubs, more animals will either live in the lot or visit it. Over a period of a year one might find a wide variety of birds, most lured by food and others by nesting sites.

Vireos are sparrow-sized birds having slightly hooked bills. They stay mainly in trees, creeping about on branches seeking insects. The most common vireo is the red-eyed vireo. As its name implies, it has a red eye. Above each eye is a black-and-white stripe.

Even more plentiful, in terms of species, are the warblers—an odd name for them since most are poor singers. These birds also spend most of their time in trees seeking insects and spiders. Unlike the slow-moving vireos, warblers flutter colorfully about. The most common is the myrtle warbler, a sparrow-sized, thin-looking bird, with a thin bill, a yellow rump and white throat. An ovenbird, a type of warbler, with brick-red cap, walks under bushes and calls *Teacher.*

Blue jays, which need no description, always make themselves known by calling out or screeching their metallic notes. Their colorful ways and energy make them the most known and visible of all the vacant lot birds.

In the winter one can often see the slate-colored junco feeding on the seeds of weeds. The slate color extends all over except for the white belly and white outer feathers of its tail. It has a pinkish bill. Quite frequently juncoes join up with flocks of sparrows.

An ovenbird

A commonly seen woodpecker is the downy woodpecker. Mostly black and white, it has a white back, a tiny red cap, and, for a woodpecker, a small bill. The hairy woodpecker looks almost exactly like the downy but is larger and has a large bill. The downy eats insects, insect eggs, and wood borers, as well as berries, nuts, acorns.

The most common mammal in a vacant lot will be unseen

by almost everyone. It is the shrew. Though at first glance a shrew resembles a mouse, it is not related and is quite different—smaller, with a more pointed head, and without the mouse's large eyes and ears. America's smallest mammal, the shrew hunts insects, grubs, and earthworms. A shrew must eat almost all the time and so must spend all its waking hours hunting for food.

The most common is the short-tailed shrew, which is only about three inches long and weighs a bit less than an ounce. To aid in its hunts it counts on its fierceness. Amazingly, it can also count on the fact that its bite is poisonous. *Never play with a shrew.* It hunts at night and roams through vacant lots in its endless search for its next meal.

Unfortunately for people who live in cities, rats are frequently found in vacant lots. In fact, the small world of a vacant lot is their ideal place. Rats prefer to spend most of their time outdoors. When night falls (and sometimes in broad daylight) they will wander about, sometimes entering and leaving sewers, hunting for litter in vacant lots, and raiding nearby garbage cans. Always keep tight lids on garbage cans so that rats cannot feed.

Most cities have huge numbers of gray squirrels. Of all the "wild" mammals they are the most commonly seen. As their numbers keep growing young squirrels must seek new places to live. This forces them into trees growing on vacant lots. Though most vacant lots are not really large enough for a squirrel's needs, it must make do.

Squirrels, which are so adapted to tree life, have found ways to use trees for their own safety. In trees they can live out of harm's way, where dogs and even cats, cannot catch them. Vacant lots, because of their small size, protect squirrels from large hawks, which cannot observe their prey well or maneuver easily in the confines of a vacant lot. Squirrels learn routes through the treetops. As they go from limb to limb, they can run long distances and never touch ground. A squirrel will thoroughly explore a route leading over the branches and learn it by heart. It will learn to run the route faster and faster. Once a route is learned, no predator can catch the squirrel. Moreover, squirrels often roam about in trees during wet days, especially during light drizzles, when the branches are nice and slippery. Hunters would hardly dare to chase squirrels for fear of slipping on a high branch and falling.

Squirrels' nests in trees are much larger than birds' nests and tend to be round. They have a front entrance and a weak place in the back. If an enemy pokes its nose into the front entrance, the squirrel can escape by bursting out through the weak place in the back.

During very cold weather a squirrel may stay curled up in its nest, using its fluffy tail much like a blanket, but the squirrel, which does not hibernate during the winter, will finally be forced out of its nest by thirst and hunger. Then it will go about its daily routines.

Of all the small worlds described in this book, the vacant lot shows most directly how we humans influence life. Vacant lots, especially the most cluttered and hopeless-looking, are our own environments. We, alone, make them harsh and ugly places.

Yet, they teach us something. They prove that life, if given half a chance, will take over any place it can—even our dirty, polluted, littered vacant lots.

·10·

A Fence Line on the Prairie

From a window of an airplane, high above the prairies of the United States and parts of Canada, one can see the flat lands stretching for miles. They go to the horizons and beyond. The first thing one realizes is that the prairies are unbelievably large. Then one notes that they are divided into countless fields, mostly square or rectangular in shape. Each field is fenced off, almost always with barbed wire. Although one cannot see the fences themselves, one can see the boundaries between fields because plants grow along the millions of miles of fences.

These fences out on the prairies form, surprisingly, a small world.

Beneath barbed wire fences there exists space enough for plants to grow: mainly tall grasses, but also large flowering plants and occasionally some wild bushes or trees. Most of the time these plants remain untouched, forgotten, and ignored. While working with plows, cultivators, and harvesters in the fields, farmers stay about ten feet away from the fences because heavy machinery can break down valuable fences. The machines and even workers can get entangled in barbed wire, so farmers carefully avoid the fence areas.

The fact that they do so is wonderful for wild plants and animals. Beneath a fence, in a refuge of safety, they can live their lives unmolested, carefree. They can form their own ecosystem, which most of the time is totally unlike that found in the nearby fields. It should be added that prairie cemeteries also remain untouched, having their own wild grasses, wild flowers, bushes, trees, and a few wild animals. Anything said here about the fence lines holds true for the cemeteries.

In one way, the fence lines indeed form a very small world, extending only about ten feet on either side of a fence. At the same time this is a large ecosystem. No one really knows how large it might be, but all the land under all the fences on the prairie states of the United States and Canada totals probably some million of acres.

Since this is a prairie ecosystem, it is dominated by grass. The fence lines often protect the original grasses of the prairies, so the fence line ecosystem is at times very much like the one that existed before the white men came. Often the only place one can hope to catch a glimpse of the original prairie is at fence lines.

North American prairies are defined by the height of their grasses. There are three types of prairies: the tallgrass, the midgrass, and the shortgrass prairies. When tallgrass prairies remain untouched, left alone, the grasses will grow to a height of between five and eight feet. On the midgrass prairies they will grow to a height of between two and four feet. On the shortgrass prairies they will grow from six inches to one foot and six inches.

The height of the grass reflects the amount of rainfall in the region. Prairies that have the heaviest rainfall also have the tallest grasses. When there is slightly more rainfall, those prairies merge with forests. On the other hand, short-grass prairies merge into deserts when rainfall decreases enough.

A prairie is a study of a land covered with grasses, though occasionally patches of wild flowers may color it. Here and there a lone bush or single tree may grow, even a grove of them, but this land is so big and so grassy that pioneers often called the prairies "a sea of grass."

Perhaps surprisingly, what we see is only half the picture. In the first six inches below the surface of most grassy places on the prairies lies a thick network of roots, bulbs, corms (an underground stem base), rhizomes, (a long horizontal stem base), and tubers, as well as their outgrowth. Below six inches there are more roots, mainly those of grass and lupines, some of which go to fourteen feet below the surface. If things were somehow tipped upside down, we'd see the roots growing higher than the grasses themselves.

The roots entwined in the soil form a firm matting called sod. It is so firm that pioneers and early settlers on the prairies often cut it into bricks with which they built sod houses.

Various animals live in the sod: insect larvae, often called grubs, earthworms, nematodes (a type of worm), sow bugs, millipedes, and mites. Carrion beetles, dung beetles, ground beetles, and other insects, such as ants, dig tunnels down into the sod. Mammals such as badgers, prairie dogs, ground squirrels, and coyotes dig holes in the soil. Snakes cannot make holes but often use them. A wide variety of bacteria, yeasts, and algae can also be found in the ground. The soil of the prairies forms another living world, rich in life.

The soil below the grasses and other plants serves another purpose. During the harsh prairie winters grasses appear to be dead. They are not. The roots stay alive even during the worst winters, for the soil above them insulates them from the cold winds that sweep brutally across the prairies. The ground freezes for only a short distance below the surface.

Let us take a close look at the tallgrass prairies and their fence-line world. They extend south from southern Manitoba, in Canada, deep into Texas. They are at their widest from central Illinois into Nebraska.

Many species of grasses and wild flowers grow on the tallgrass prairie. When the prairie is undisturbed, however, and allowed to remain for a period of years without being plowed (as for example, under a fence), it will be covered mainly by only two or three species of grasses. All other grasses and wild flowers and trees will play a very minor role.

The grass that dominates the tallgrass prairies is big bluestem grass *(Andropogon gerardi)*. We must use the scientific name here because this species of grass has many common names, such as turkeyfoot, bluejoint, beard grass, and others that can cause confusion.

It is called big bluestem grass because it will grow to a height of about eight feet. The stem of the grass has on it a waxlike substance called a bloom, which is either purplish or bluish in color. It is sometimes called turkeyfoot grass because the spikes that hold the flowers (these flowers do not look like most flowers because, like all grass flowers, they lack petals and are different in other ways) and later seeds are often three-pronged and resemble a turkey's foot. On occasion, a grass plant may have more prongs. The leaves, which grow from about fourteen to sixteen inches in length, have very rough edges. The surfaces, however, are soft and hairy. Big bluestem grass grows on level land if the land is well drained. It prefers to grow on the lower slopes of hills.

Grasses such as big bluestem take over and dominate because they have several advantages over other plants and grasses. They are long-lived—they can live to be twenty years old—and once they grow they establish themselves and consequently keep other plants away for long periods of time. During their long lifetime individual plants can continue to spread by means of roots and seeds. As the plant spreads it conquers more territory for itself. The dominant plants tend to be big both in height and volume. Most can, if necessary, grow in the shade. This allows them to grow up among wild flowers and even in the shade of trees.

Prairie grasses are extremely well adapted to life on the prairie. For example, bluestem grass, though tall, is flexible and if necessary can bend continuously in the wind for days on end. The grass needs the wind so that it can reproduce itself. Pollens move in the wind from one grass to another and fertilize seeds, which will also be scattered by the winds. Prairie grasses are plants of the wind. Nothing is more beautiful than seeing sun-filled fields of ripe grass rippling green and free in the wind.

The leaves of prairie grasses grow vertically and so receive less sunlight than the leaves of most wild flowers, whose leaves are usually horizontal. The fact that much of the plant is nothing but leaves compensates for this. Grasses growing together receive more sunlight than single isolated plants. This is so because sunlight reflects off grasses to the leaves of other grasses. Prairie grasses can withstand the cold winters, too, because their roots are protected underground and can send up new shoots. Nor are they harmed by the raging wildfires that occasionally sweep across the prairies. In many ways grasses are ideally suited for life on the open, sunny, windy prairies. It is because they are so well adapted to the open lands that they have become so numerous. Actually more land in the United States is covered by grass than by any other type of plant. Thirty-eight percent of the land south of Canada is covered with grasses, as is much of southern Canada.

Although the big bluestem dominates the tallgrass prairies, it rarely grows alone. It is almost always found growing with some other species, the most common of which are needlegrass, Kentucky bluegrass, and Indian grass. Needlegrass is easy to identify. The upper parts of the leaves are corrugated, but the underside is shiny-green and smooth. Its seeds have long thin "needlelike" projections.

Kentucky bluegrass, contrary to popular belief, probably did not originate in Kentucky. It has mysterious origins. No one even knows if it is native to America or was brought here by Europeans. To identify it, look at the tips of its leaves. They are boat-shaped. The flowering head resembles, in a way, a scraggly Christmas tree—that is to say, it is pyramidal in shape, very open and delicate-looking.

Indian grass, like big bluestem, is a tall grass, and might easily be mistaken for big bluestem. However, the spike of flowers and seeds at the top of the grass is very different. It is not forked as is big bluestem; the grass terminates with just one big fluffy spike. Indian grass can be identified by its **ligules.** If you look at the place where the leaf joins the stem, you will see that on Indian grass there are two hornlike projections, called ligules, where stem and leaf meet. Each ligule is paper-thin and hairless.

The mix of grasses on the prairies is rarely the same as it was before white men entered the region. Environmental changes have taken place.

As farmers plow fields for wheat, corn, and other crops, the native plants are destroyed. Billions of individual plants are killed by farm equipment each year. The more delicate species of plants, the slower-growing species, and those that were never great in numbers die off first.

The selective eating of cattle has also affected the type of plants we see on the prairie. Cattle prefer big bluestem grass to any other kind. They also like to eat legumes, plants of the pea family. If cattle graze in a field of grasses and flowering plants, they will eat away the big bluestem and legumes first. Because they dislike goldenrods and asters, they leave these to the last, until they are almost starving.

Fence lines protect trees and shrubs. Frequently one can see lines of trees crossing the prairies, growing next to fences. The most common are hawthorn trees. Only an expert botanist can tell one species of hawthorn from another, but they are mostly small and many appear to be more like shrubs than trees. All have small red berries and thorny branches.

The bur oak is seen too, one of the very few oaks that can manage life on the prairies. The leaves of bur oaks are indented, smoothly lobed. The top of the leaf is the thickest part. The oak's acorns are half covered with very hairy cups, and the bark is deeply furrowed.

The Kentucky coffee tree is never common. It is a scraggly tree, whose twigs are scaly. Identify it by the large, broad bean and furrowed bark. Folklore has it that the beans have been used, at times, as coffee substitutes, and that explains its name. It's been said that not even a magician could make coffee from the beans.

Siberian elms, which originated in Asia, are grown in order to slow down the fierce winds of the prairies that carry away topsoil.

Many prairie plant species that were once common are rare today, but fortunately they can sometimes be found, protected, under barbed wire fences. Among such plants are the leadplant, flowering spurge, false boneset, ground plum, showy tick trefoil, tooth-leaved primrose, wild licorice, and prairie clover. They still bloom out on the prairies thanks to fences and graveyards.

Leadplants are flowering shrubs that grow to a height of about three feet. They are grayish-looking and have flowers of an intense blue color growing in thick, spike-shaped clusters. Oddly, though of the pea family, the flowers each have only one petal. The leaves are covered with white-gray hairs. The roots of the plant can reach four feet underground, allowing the plant to compete with deep-rooted grasses for moisture. The plant got its odd name because at one time people believed that these plants indicated soils that contained lead-bearing minerals.

Flowering spurge grows to be about three feet high. The bottom part of the plant rises on a single stem, but it branches off into flower stems and oval leaves. The flowers have white bracts, which appear to be five "petals."

Showy tick trefoil grows to be six feet high. The flowers, like most other flowers of the pea family, have five petals. Two of the lower ones are joined to form a drooping lip.

The stem and seedpods are hairy, and the oval leaves grow in groups of three.

Wild licorice comes in two varieties, one that has greenish-white flowers and one that has yellow flowers. Both plants grow to be about two feet high. Look for the four broad, oval-shaped leaves. Four leaves at a time grow from the stem, forming crosslike patterns. The flowers are small.

Today some very rare plants, such as mead's milkweed, can also on occasion be found, usually under fences.

The plants found at fences lines are not the only survivors of the past. Quite a number of animals also benefit from the peaceful life there. Some find cover among the wild plants beneath the fences; others eat the seeds, berries, fruit, and roots of the fence line plants.

Many birds build nests along fence lines in the grasses, weeds, shrubs, and trees. They find the wires and posts good perches. In fact, the best places to see birds in the prairies is on fences and fence posts. Some are migrants that fly north in the spring and south in the autumn. Others live on the plains most of the year, and some all year long.

The male indigo bunting is a dark-blue bird about the size of an English sparrow. (The female is brown and difficult to identify.) It nests in tangles and shrubs along fence lines. Since these birds often perch on fence wires, one is able to see them.

A field sparrow is the only sparrow with a pink bill and reddish cap. It is more often heard than seen. Its song sounds like *twee, twee, twee, te, te, te, te, te, te.* Unlike almost all other birds, it often sings in the moonlight.

The grasshopper sparrow can be identified by its short tail, far shorter than that of other sparrows. Its breast is buff in color and lacking any markings. It runs like a mouse on the ground and when it flies usually stays close to the ground. It sings mainly while perched on weed stalks. Its song, which has an insectlike buzz *(tit-zeeeeee),* is often loud enough to be heard from a slow-moving automobile.

A true bird of the prairie, not seen anyplace else in the United States, is the Harris sparrow. One can easily identify it by the fact that it is our only sparrow having a black cap, face, and throat. It often forages on the ground, but it will sing from a perch and can be heard on moonlit nights. Listen for its alarm note, a loud *wink.*

A Harris sparrow

A Swainson's hawk often perches on fence posts. One can identify this medium-sized hawk by the fact that, unlike other hawks, it has a dark breast and pale belly. When it flies, you can see that the leading edges of its wings are light-colored and the back edges dark-colored. It usually flies low, holding its wings in a V shape, hunting for ground squirrels, gophers, rats, and grasshoppers. Its cry is *kreeeeee.*

Many mammals also live around the fences. One is the grasshopper mouse. This small animal is ferocious for its size. It attacks and kills grasshoppers and even scorpions, small lizards, and other mice. The grasshopper mouse rarely weighs more than an ounce. It has white undersides, a short tail, and smaller ears than most mice.

Thirteen-lined ground squirrels, which have thirteen lightly colored stripes on their backs, live in tunnels. Often one hears its whistle before seeing the animal. These ground squirrels have black stripes and white dots on their backs. Their horizontal tunnels, which may extend more than twenty feet, begin and end hidden in vegetation, often that found under fences. They eat plants, seeds, berries, tubers, and roots, as well as grasshoppers and other insects.

During the winter these ground squirrels hibernate—that is, they sleep very deeply, so deeply that their body temperature falls dramatically and their heartbeat has a very slow pace. In the more southern parts of the prairies, they **estivate** during hot summer months. Estivation is a summer hibernation, when these rodents lie deep underground in their cool tunnels trying to escape the heat.

Another prairie-fence animal is the American badger, a large, black-and-white mammal that lives in a burrow. For their size, these mammals are exceptionally tough, fierce fighters. One badger can fight off several dogs. Badgers often hunt thirteen-lined ground squirrels and will dig up the length of a twenty-foot tunnel just to corner a squirrel.

Bull snakes, often called gopher snakes, and rattlesnakes, are typical prairie snakes. They hunt rodents, birds, lizards, and other snakes. A bull snake grows to about five feet in length, the only snake with forty-one to sixty-five square black blotches on a yellow ground.

In looks and color rattlesnakes often vary a great deal from place to place, but they can be easily identified by the rattles on their tails. Needless to say, rattlesnakes are dangerous and one should always watch out for them.

The fence lines and cemeteries in preserving the natural prairie, serve as accidental refuges for plants and wildlife. Some animals and plants now preserved by the fences may some day prove to be of great value in an as yet undiscovered way. Many, if not all, of our commercial crops were once just "weeds."

An example can be given of a weed that became valuable during recent times. During World War II, when cork could not be obtained for desperately needed life preservers, tufts of common milkweed seeds were used instead. Many people survived ship sinkings because their life jackets were stuffed with tufts from just a plain old ordinary weed.

In recent years four plants considered to be weeds have become major crops: buffalo gourds of the North American deserts are grown for their rich seeds filled with oils and proteins as well as for the starch in their roots; jojoba of Mexico is grown for its oil, which is like that valuable oil found in sperm whales. The use of this oil can save those whales. Crambe of the Mediterranean countries produces erucic acid used in plasticizers. Kenaf of East Africa is used for making paper, thus saving countless valuable trees.

Other weeds that will be soon used include *Cuphea* for fatty acids, bladderpod for a valuable machine oil, guayule for rubber, and gumweed for adhesives.

Who knows what plants and animals that take refuge beneath fence lines will some day be useful to us in ways we cannot even dream of? Meanwhile we have the joy of sharing this planet with beautiful and fascinating living things.

·11·

Roadsides

If you go for a long drive, you will eventually see ditches along the sides of roads. As workers build roads, they take dirt from the roadside and place it where the road will be. This lifts the finished road, so that water will drain off it and the road will be drier and safer.

When a road goes along the side of a hillside, part of the hill must be cut away for the roadway. This leaves a steep embankment on the side of the road. If the road cuts through a small hill, there will be two embankments, one on each side, plus ditches at the base of the embankments.

The ditches and embankments form a small world, unlike that of the fields, woods, and countryside just beyond. Plants and animals of the roadside will often be noticeably different from those found even a few feet away.

Let's take a look at this commonly seen and easily found small ecosystem.

The roadside ecosystem is really two systems, which in many ways are very different. Plants in general find the ditches an easier place to live. Left untouched, ditches will often have many more species of plants than embankments. If there is a steady supply of water along a ditch, there may even be aquatic plants, as well as frogs, and in southern Atlantic coast states, the greater siren salamander.

Most embankments are rather barren areas. Road crews usually keep them clear of trees and dense shrubs so that drivers can see the road ahead. If you look at an embankment, you will see mainly weeds and at times spectacular wild flowers.

Since embankments are usually steep—some being very steep indeed—rainwater quickly drains off of them. This means that many embankments are very dry. They can be desertlike, especially if they face toward the south. Consequently plants on embankments meet challenges. They must endure the direct rays of the sun and high winds sweeping across the open roadside. Embankments cut through hills often act as funnels that increase high winds. Dust and pollution from passing cars and trucks pose hazards. Rainwater gushes down embankments, loosening soil and damaging roots. In the wintertime salt put on the road to melt ice gets into the soil, making it difficult for plants to grow. In the end many of these plants, so unwanted, are cut away by road crews as they clear embankments.

It is amazing that anything at all grows on embankments. Yet plants struggle to live there. Those that can withstand the conditions manage it quite well. Most plants that grow on embankments and in ditches are annuals. These are typically flowering plants that grow from seeds. They flower, produce seeds for next year's plants, and then die away. The plants themselves never live more than a single period of time, from spring to autumn. Most roadside plants must be annuals because the road crews usually clear them out each year. If road crews neglect an area for a few years, a few plants will be perennial, living for more than one year and often several years.

Interestingly, many of the plants that bloom on embankments attract our attention because of their spectacular flowers and because they grow to be several feet in height. These dramatic plants often attract a wide variety of insects. Since these plants are considered to be nuisance weeds, no one sprays them with insecticides. Costly insecticides go on crops, not on weeds, so the plants on the embankments and in the ditches are "organic." Insects can safely visit them to sip nectar without being killed.

Once the flowers produce seeds, usually in late summer and in the autumn, birds and rodents will go to roadside areas to eat them. In the winter, some of the best high fat and protein food available to birds and mammals will be roadside seeds. Grasses also grow beside the roads, both on the embankments and in the ditches, and these too produce seeds of great food value.

As often as not, animals will be more interested in feeding along the roadside than in the fields of farmers. Field crops produce flowers and seeds all at once during given periods of time, which tend to be short, only a week or so. In contrast, roadside plants produce flowers and seeds continuously from spring through autumn and even through the winter. Animals visit ditches, too, to drink water or bathe; even dry and dusty ditches provide dust baths for birds.

Wherever animals, large or small, gather, predators will surely seek them out. Plant-eating animals spend their lives being hunted by predators. The animals of roadsides are no exception. (One can often see hunters such as hawks from the window of an automobile; in fact, one can often see them better that way than hiking about in fields and forests.) So the small world has its own food chain. The annuals feed animals with their nectar and seeds. These animals in turn are hunted by predators from wolf spiders to large hawks and long snakes.

Some animals such as woodchucks find that embankments are good places to dig holes and make dens. Salamanders and frogs will find ditchwater a good place to lay eggs. So will mosquitoes and other insects. Fence posts, signposts, and fence wires that border roadsides make excellent perching places for hawks as well as for large flocks of migrating birds. All these activities can easily be seen from the windows of a car or bus.

Among the roadside annuals, which people often call weeds, are mulleins (from the Latin word, meaning "wooly"). This plant is tall and has large, thick, furry leaves. It has a single dramatic spike, which grows from two to six feet in height. In the summer one can see rather undramatic-looking yellow flowers, each with five petals. The flowers are not important food supplies for insects or other animals.

During the winter the mullein's spikes remain. The thick leaves fall down and cover the ground. Many insects hibernate in these wooly, cozy leaves. In fact, mulleins help countless insects survive the winter. For this reason mulleins are important to the small ecosystem.

Early goldenrod has lovely feathery plumes of yellow flowers and thin, toothless upper leaves. A near relative, rough-stemmed goldenrod, grows very tall, reaching at times a height of seven feet. Unlike the early goldenrod, it has leaves that have deep teeth along the edges. It blooms in late summer and autumn. These plants would be enjoyed by all if they were not a major cause of hay fever.

We think of plants as having colorful flowers, but dock is a weed that has green-to brown-colored flowers. The seeds, which are surrounded by three papery "wings," are a tobacco-brown color. Birds feed on them.

A commonly seen roadside plant, pigweed, may produce tens of thousands of seeds in a season, serving as a huge reservoir of food for many birds, insects, and some mammals. If we consider all the roads in the United States, their area would be about the size of the state of Georgia, so the roadside "small world" is in a sense a very large world. In terms of food for wild animals, pigweeds go a long way toward making it a productive world.

Teasel is a very large weed, which has an unusual flower head. It is egg-shaped, covered with spines, and in a way looks like a pincushion. The stem is covered with small thorns. Teasels may grow to be six feet tall. At one time they were grown as crops because the teasels were used as combs for combing out wool.

The teasel is an interesting example of why we should hesitate to call any plant a weed. At one time it was a valued plant and grown as a crop. Today it is weed. Who knows, tomorrow it may again find value. Any weed might become a valued food crop, a source of medicine, a renewable fuel. On the other hand, certain valued plants today may become weeds in the future.

On rocky slopes one might see fire pinks. The five petals of these scarlet flowers are notched at their tips. The flowers grow on long stalks.

One can find many thistles, but Canada thistles are the most common. The plants have numerous smallish lilac-colored flowers, which are quite fragrant. The plant grows to a height of five feet. It has many branches, which unlike other thistles, are hairless. So are the leaves.

Blue vervain plants are topped with many flowering heads that stand up like candles in branching candlesticks. The flowers are bluish purple.

A fire pink

Horseweeds grow to seven feet in height. They have numerous stalks and leaves and many, many small green flowers. These weeds, which are rank, grow almost everywhere and produce tremendous numbers of seeds, which contribute greatly to the basic food supply of the ecosystem.

Milkweeds also grow along roadsides (see Chapter Three). Bindweeds, which look like morning glories, climb fence posts, telephone poles, and signposts along highways and roads. Small clovers are common.

All these weeds and many others supply the necessary

food base for the roadside world and, in the case of the mulleins, winter homes for insects.

Taking advantage of the flowering annuals are, first, the insects, which sip nectar from the blooming flowers. Those insects that visit the flowers are mainly bumblebees, honeybees, butterflies, and moths.

Many swallowtails, which are the largest American butterflies, may be seen at Queen Anne's lace, a medium-tall

Bindweed

plant topped with a flat cluster of flowers. The middle tiny flower is often reddish, purplish, even black in color. The plant is a **biennial;** it lives only two years.

The swallowtails seen on the flowers are black swallowtails.

Coppers, medium-sized butterflies often copper-red in color, can often be seen flitting about near roadsides. Honey- and bumblebees also visit roadside plants.

Waiting for all of them are the predators. Spiders have their webs ready in case an insect lands in them. Crab spiders hide in flowers waiting to grasp any insect that gets within range of its legs. Ladybugs crawl about on the plants searching for insects. On the ground wolf spiders look for prey. Once a victim is seen, the wolf spider runs it down.

A black swallowtail butterfly

Bugs suck juices out of leaves and stems. Leaf-eating beetles and grasshoppers will eat the leaves. In the late summer and fall, insects such as milkweed bugs will eat the seeds. From flowering to seeds the weeds and wild flowers will be under attack as hordes of insects feed on them. At the same time the insects themselves will be killed by birds or predator insects.

Meadowlarks can be seen near roadsides. These robin-sized birds often perch on fence posts and sing their beautiful song, which sounds like *spring-o'-the-YEar.* Like many birds they eat insects when insects are most plentiful and at other times they eat seeds and grains.

Eastern kingbirds also perch on fence posts and fences,

darting out to catch flying insects. It has a white band at the end of its tail. The brave kingbird will attack crows, even hawks, sometimes riding on their backs.

Horned larks are small birds that have tiny, hard-to-see "horns" on their heads. These "horns" are, of course, tufts of feathers. The larks stay in flocks, and when disturbed they shoot upward and circle around, often landing again where they took off. As they fly one can see their white underparts and black tails. These birds stay in grass fields and roadsides. Unlike most birds, they *walk* rather than hop. They mainly eat seeds, but insects make about up 20 percent of their diet.

A meadow lark

Three types of blue birds often stay near roadsides: blue grosbeaks, indigo buntings, and actual bluebirds. From a car one would have trouble telling them apart.

Mockingbirds are the only birds with long tails and white

patches on their wings. As they fly one can see the patches. They sing all sorts of songs, which they learn from other birds. They eat insects, seeds, and berries.

Common crows not only eat insects, seeds, and berries but will also eat animals newly killed by automobiles. One will see them feasting in the middle of a road. In the West, one sees ravens, which look like larger crows, do the same.

Rodents are attracted to the seeds of grasses and flowers. Most are field mice of one species or another.

The birds and mammals attract mosquitoes. Female mosquitoes will suck their blood so that the mosquito eggs will develop.

Also waiting for the mice and, rarely, for the birds will be the hawks. A roadside is a good place for hawks. There is always a sign, a pole, and fence post to perch on. The view is clear and open. Sharp-shinned hawks mainly hunt birds up to the size of pigeons but will eat rodents and insects as well. These hawks have broad, rounded wings but long, square tails. Their backs are dark gray and their breasts have many narrow reddish-brown bands. In flight they are swift and sure.

The Cooper's hawk looks almost identical to the sharp-shinned hawk but is much larger. Its tail is more rounded and it may have a wingspan of twenty-eight inches. It can kill duck-sized birds.

The rough-legged hawk has very wide wings, a short black tail with a white band, and a black belly. It is a large hawk and can have a wingspread of fifty-two inches. In spite of its size, it lacks the speed and fierce nature of the Cooper's hawk. It mainly eats rodents, especially mice. This somewhat uncommon hawk may be seen perched on posts in meadows.

The red-tailed hawk can have a wingspan of forty-eight inches. Identify it by its red tail. It is rather commonly seen perched in open areas and eats mainly rodents.

The most common hawk is a small one, the sparrow hawk. It is also the most beautiful. Identify it by its red-black-and-white head. It has a wingspan of twenty-one inches. It mainly eats mice, insects, and sparrow-sized birds. Quite often its distinctive cry can be heard: *killy, killy, killy.*

Snakes also come to roadsides to hunt. Rough green snakes have ridges on their scales and can reach a length of four feet. They come to hunt insects, spiders, and six-lined racerunner lizards.

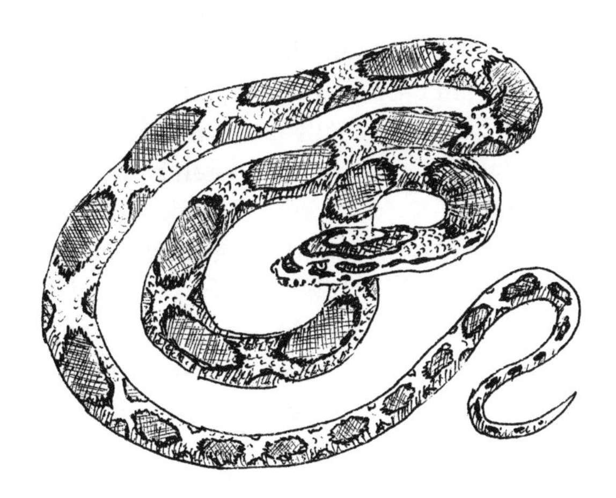

A corn snake

The corn snake, a big snake varying in color from reddish-brown to yellow, with saddle-shaped red blotches, is thought by some to be the most beautiful snake in the world. It eats rodents, birds, and lizards.

The prairie king snake, as long as fifty inches, has dark reddish-brown blotches on its back and dark blotches on its yellow belly. It attacks rodents, lizards, and smaller snakes.

The six-lined racerunner lizard can be identified by its very long tail. It is a study in speed, making fast stops and starts, often sticking out its tongue. It hunts insects and spiders.

These numerous types of roadside hunters tell us something about the amount of food the plants produce for insects, birds, and rodents. Roadside areas are far more productive in terms of plants and animals than they appear to be.

Occasionally one will also see woodchucks near a road. They sometimes live in holes that they have dug in road embankments. These mammals, about as large as cocker spaniels, have small ears and tails. They eat roadside plants such as clover. During the winter, they hibernate inside grass-lined tunnels. Look for woodchucks in early morning and late afternoon.

In today's world animals are threatened not only by hunter animals but by another powerful killer—the automobile. It is virtually impossible to drive a hundred miles, or at times even one mile, during the summer without killing numerous insects. On occasion a car will hit a mouse or a rabbit or another roadside mammal. Once in a while a speeding automobile might even hit a roadside bird.

The roadside world—for passengers, not drivers—can be fascinating. It is varied and filled with life—more than can be spelled out in a small book like this. Most of all, one can, in a comfortable way, see nature in action.

Glossary

ANNUAL. A flowering plant that sprouts, flowers, produces seeds, and dies all within a year. See *biennial, perennial.*

BIENNIAL. A flowering plant that bears seeds the first year and dies in the second. See *annual, perennial.*

BRACTS. Special leaves, almost always highly colored, which attract insects because they look like flowers.

CAPSULE. A spore container. See *spore*, *sori*, and *sporophyte.*

CARNIVORE. An animal or plant that eats live flesh. See *herbivore, omnivore.*

CHLOROPHYLL. A green chemical compound that is essential to photosynthesis in plants. It reacts with light energy, carbon dioxide, and water to form sugars and other carbohydrates. See *photosynthesis.*

CLIMAX PLANTS. When a particular ecosystem or small world has gone through a succession of different groups of plants over a period of time from a few years to centuries, it finally stabilizes. At that time, the final groups of plants will appear. No other groups of plants will occur. These final plants are called the climax plants. (See the chapters on dunes, cliffs, and vacant lots.)

COMMENSALISM. In biology this refers to a relationship in which a species of animal eats food left over from the meals of another species of animal. House mice, for example, share a commensal relationship with humans.

COMMUNITIES. Another name for small worlds, small ecosystems. This book is about communities.

ECOSYSTEM. A network of relationships between the nonliving environment—factors such as soil and climate—and living organisms. An ecosystem can be big—the world, for example—or small, such as the small worlds described in this book.

ESTIVATE. To sleep for days or even weeks in a cool hole or other place during the hot part of a summer. See *hibernate.*

EVOLUTION. Over long periods of time—millions of years—plants and animals change their shapes, way of life, and bodily chemistry. Evolution is the process of those changes.

FOOD CHAIN. In each ecosystem or small world there is a food chain, which describes who eats whom. Almost all food chains start with plants and end with predators. Animals that eat only plants are said to be low on a food chain. The predator that is not eaten by any other animal is the highest member of a food chain.

HERBIVORE. An animal that eats only plants. See *carnivore, omnivore.*

HERMAPHRODITE. An animal, such as some snails, that has both male and female sex organs.

HIBERNATE. To sleep for weeks in a protected place such as a den during the cold winter months.

HYDROPHYTE. A plant having special types of leaves, roots, and inner chemistry that allow it to live in very damp places—even in the water at times.

LARVA. Different insect species go through different stages as they grow. A butterfly, for example, is first in an egg. Once it hatches, a caterpillar appears, which is a larva. It later becomes a butterfly. Maggots, for example, are fly larvae.

LIGULES. A thin appendage, often scale-like, that appears on many species of grasses. The position, shape, and size of ligules can often help one identify different species of grasses.

NYMPH. Some insects—for example, cinch bugs and spittle bugs—hatch directly as nymphs that resemble small adults.

They will grow to be adults. In other words, these insects do not go through a larval stage. See *larva.*

OMNIVORE. An animal that eats both plants and the flesh of animals. See *carnivore, herbivore.*

PALMATE. Some leaf clusters are termed palmate. This means that the separate leaves in the cluster radiate outward from a common point. Such a cluster resembles fingers on a hand.

PERENNIAL. Flowering plants that live longer than two years and produce new growth and seeds each year. See *annual, biennial.*

PHOTOSYNTHESIS. A chemical process by which plants make sugar and other carbohydrates with chlorophyll, carbon dioxide, water, and the energy of sunlight (as well as some types of artificial light). Plants later use the carbohydrates for their own nourishment. See *chlorophyll.*

POLLEN. The dust produced on flowers. It contains the male reproductive sperm, which can fertilize a flower so seeds will develop and later sprout.

POLYPORE FUNGI. Many fungi species, called polypores, are frequently found as shelf fungus on trees. Some are brightly colored, but most are brick red, brown, and white. They cause dry rot, which reduces wood to a powder.

PREDATOR. An animal that hunts and kills other animals for food.

RHIZOID. Primitive plants, such as lichens and liverworts, lack true roots—that is, roots that absorb water through tubes. Instead they attach themselves to rocks, trees, and soil by means of simple rhizoids, which do not absorb water.

SETA. The stalk of a sporophyte.

SORI. Sori capsules look like small buttons on the leaves of ferns. They hold fern spore. Once the sori burst, spore drift away in the wind and new fern plants develop from them. Many ferns are identified by the shape and location of sori.

SPORE. A dustlike reproductive grain capable of forming new individual plants. It is found on many primitive plants such as mosses and ferns.

SPOROPHYTES. These special reproductive organs found on

mosses make spores. Sporophytes consist of a stalk, called a seta, and a capsule.

STOMATA. Leaves must have openings in them so that necessary gases, such as carbon dioxide and oxygen, as well as water vapor, can enter and leave. Such holes, which are too small on most leaves to be seen without a magnifying glass, are called stomata.

SYMBIOSIS. A mutually beneficial relationship between two plants or animals of different species is called a symbiotic relationship. For example, lichen and fungi can live together to form another plant. A person and a dog form a symbiotic relationship that benefits both. During a symbiotic relationship the process of symbiosis takes place.

THALLI (singular: Thallus). The leaf-like growth of primitive plants. Flowering plants and conifers have true leaves; since thalli lack veins and other structures found in the leaves of higher plants, they are not true leaves.

XEROPHYTE. A plant that has special types of leaves (or totally lacks leaves), roots, and inner chemistry that allow it to live in such dry places as dunes and deserts.

Index